ADVANCE PRAISE FOR

White Evolution: The Constant Struggle for Racial Consciousness

"My first reaction upon reading the introduction to *White Evolution* was 'wow' because even though I still had much work to do I could not stop myself from reading. There is a lot of talk about diversity, inclusivity, and equity but hardly any talk about the many ways in which Whiteness is implicated in the structures, practices, and mindsets. *White Evolution* shows the many sides of Whiteness illustrated with compelling stories that make it hard to stop reading. The authors also share their own personal experiences with Whiteness which will help readers understand their own fears and apprehensions and learn to see and talk about Whiteness naturally. This is an excellent book for higher education practitioners and leaders."

—Estela Mara Bensimon, Ph.D.
Professor, University of Southern California

"*White Evolution* tackles some of the most urgent social and political issues of our time. Grounded in rich historical context and complex critical analysis, this book provides a powerful discussion of the evolution of White racial consciousness. It is a must-read for anyone seeking to understand how race and Whiteness operate and how we can collectively evolve to produce a more racially equitable society."

—Samuel D. Museus, Ph.D.
Professor, University of California, San Diego

White Evolution

This book is part of the Peter Lang Education list.
Every volume is peer reviewed and meets the highest
quality standards for content and production.

PETER LANG
New York • Bern • Berlin
Brussels • Vienna • Oxford • Warsaw

Christopher S. Collins and Alexander Jun

White Evolution

The Constant Struggle for Racial Consciousness

PETER LANG
New York • Bern • Berlin
Brussels • Vienna • Oxford • Warsaw

Library of Congress Control Number: 2020937507

Bibliographic information published by **Die Deutsche Nationalbibliothek**.
Die Deutsche Nationalbibliothek lists this publication in the "Deutsche
Nationalbibliografie"; detailed bibliographic data are available
on the Internet at http://dnb.d-nb.de/.

ISBN 978-1-4331-7607-4 (hardcover)
ISBN 978-1-4331-7608-1 (paperback)
ISBN 978-1-4331-7609-8 (ebook pdf)
ISBN 978-1-4331-7610-4 (epub)
ISBN 978-1-4331-7611-1 (mobi)
DOI 10.3726/b16361

Cover images: engraving: ©iStock.com/bauhaus1000; brain: ©iStock.com/Ryzhi

The paper in this book meets the guidelines for permanence and durability
of the Committee on Production Guidelines for Book Longevity
of the Council of Library Resources.

© 2020 Peter Lang Publishing, Inc., New York
29 Broadway, 18th floor, New York, NY 10006
www.peterlang.com

Printed in the United States of America

We dedicate this book to our family and friends, who provided just the right amount of challenge and support we needed to accomplish this worthwhile endeavor.

For Kristy, Mateo, and Adela:

May we be peacemakers, justice-seekers, and messengers.

—Christopher S. Collins

For Jeany, Natalia, Isaiah, and Jeremiah: Do justice. Love mercy. Walk humbly.

—Alexander Jun

We would also like to dedicate this work to the Social Justice and Diversity Fellowship recipients at the Ph.D. program in higher education at Azusa Pacific University. All of the author proceeds from this publication will go to enhance the fellowship program to support students pursuing doctoral studies and pursuing social justice.

CONTENTS

FIGURES

PREFACE

A substantial amount of writing has been published in recent years on White supremacy, privilege, and racism, with some overlaps. Some offer a new spin on previous work, while others offer a response to the plethora of current events that receive conventional and social media coverage. It can be hard to discern what to read or what tool to use, but of this we are certain—there is consistent exposure of White supremacist violence that is revealed in new and advanced ways every day. Each blog, article, or book that addresses White supremacy is imperfect, incomplete, and quickly becomes old news. As a result, we continue the struggle for racial consciousness and appreciate the fact that each person or group working in anti-racism has a different sphere of influence. In this book we present the concept of White evolution as a way to cultivate critical racial consciousness, with the hope of having a portable concept in an ever-evolving racialized society.

Is Race Real?

Race is a difficult concept. In a superficial way, we have heard people make the argument that the real problem is *talking* so much about race. People of all races express fatigue with the topic and resist the dialogue by criticizing the discussion as the problem. We liken that logic to saying, "*talking* about a virus is the problem," as opposed to acknowledging the virus itself is a problem. In truth, race exists because of racism.

Some very thoughtful educators and scholars have advocated against the continued perpetuation of the use of race. For example, Brian Bantum in the book *The Death of Race* makes a very in-depth and nuanced argument that because race has produced death, then race must die.[1] But race will not go away just because the term or discussion ceases to exist. Race is a byproduct of racism, and the enduring nature of racism ensures its persistence.

Advocating for the discontinued use of racial categories may come with good intentions but may unintentionally be coupled with a shallow version of colorblindness. Ignoring race may White out someone's affinity and identity as Black or Latinx. Consider Jane Elliott—champion and pioneer of the blue eyes/brown eyes experiment which was featured on the PBS original *A Class Divided* in 1985.[2] In 2019 she appeared on an episode of *Red Table Talk* with Jada Pinkett Smith (as well as Jada's mother, daughter, and a producer who is a White woman).[3] Prior to Jane joining the conversation, the women discussed the relationship between White women and women of color. They discussed the role of trust, assumptions, and history. Jada's mother had just expressed the greatest challenges in working with White women when in the last six minutes of the episode, they brought out Jane Elliot, who was wearing a sweatshirt proclaiming:

> God created one race
> THE HUMAN RACE
> Human beings created racism

During her short appearance on the episode, she shared provocative thoughts about her current stance on race, with her usual sense of gravitas and force. After giving a brief history lesson, she said: "I'm not a White woman, I'm a faded Black person. That's all any White person is." Jada's face looked stunned as Jane quickly went on to back up her point.

Jane used the platform to advance the idea that the problem is the *belief* in and continued use of race (sustained by racist institutions, including school systems). So, the solution is to discontinue the belief in and use of race. As a test to see if her listeners around the table got the quick lesson, she said, "If you are biracial stand up." A couple of the women stood up and Jane almost exploded, banged her hand on the table, and said "I told you there is only ONE race. Didn't you listen to anything I said?"

In all fairness, Jane Elliot had certainly earned the right to share her opinion. She has witnessed and endured more than most in the confrontation of White supremacy, but her commitment to this particular position seemed off. It took us a while to figure out why. We are grateful for Elliott and all she has accomplished in her many years of conducting workshops and consciousness raising with adults and especially children. We disagree with her premise in this brief appearance, not just because the social construction of race is still a felt, real, and lived experience that people of color know daily, with painful consequences. The main reason for our discomfort was her disposition. It was the way she interacted with the people of color around her. She asked no questions, showed no humility, and did not engage in dialogue. She launched an idea, pushed it, tested her listeners on whether they had learned it, and left no room for cultural humility. Toward the end of her appearance, she forcefully pointed to the table and said, "Blacks and people of color have got to stop playing defense and got to start playing offense." Even a brave woman like Jane Elliott is, at the end of the day, still White and perpetuating White logic.

The brief vignette is an apt precursor for understanding our main premise regarding White evolution as a constant struggle for racial consciousness. Jane, a White woman, sat before Black women and gave them a lesson in eradicating race. Unintentionally, this advocate for anti-racism advanced truth with the veracity of Whiteness. Her White truth, that race does not exist, is another White lie. When we stop evolving, challenging, and pursuing critical racial consciousness, our ideas stagnate. When we become convinced that our ideas are the best and we shut out other voices from conversation, our sustenance from interdependence declines. When we are proud in a way that diminishes someone else, and when we lack the cultural humility to engage with critical feedback, our souls become stale.

White Evolution

Two fundamental and underlying principles drive this book. The first is that the evolution of racial consciousness requires a constant drive in the fight against the virus of White supremacy. If the virus is evolving rapidly, then our critical consciousness needs to evolve faster in order to outpace the supremacy. The second is that this evolution is not an individual act—it must be done in community through collective critical racial consciousness. The genetic makeup of human beings points to the necessity of interdependence.

Growth and development do not lead to a solitary life so much as to being a dependable person rooted in community. The origin of White supremacy, conversely, is entrenched in reproducing uniformity and eradicating diversity. In an ecological framework, uniformity and monoculture are harmful to an ecosystem that needs diversity of thought, creativity, culture, perspective, history, and economy to survive. The White supremacy intended to *preserve a pure race* has created an enduring system of violence against people of color and is simultaneously hurting the endurability of humanity in exchange for the immediate gains of supremacy.

In terms of context for the book, we believe that White supremacy is a *system* with many evolving manifestations. The key word for us is *system*. It is not all about White people. Layla Saad, author of the "Me and White Supremacy Workbook," wrote the guided journey for individuals who carry White privilege.[4] In the workbook, she explains that White privilege is held by those who are visually identifiable as White, White-passing, or holding White privilege.

Saad offers a powerful guided journey and ventures into some complexity by addressing biracial, mixed race, and people of color who hold White privilege because they have visibly lighter skin than Black, Brown, and Indigenous peoples. We agree with Saad's ideas, and we also think that White supremacy related to people of color goes beyond skin tone and passing as White. There have always been non-skin color markers of race that give people additional access to benefiting from White systems—even if they are not White. Which leads us to a major commitment of the book: focusing on systems in addition to individuals. White logic is a unique interaction between individuals and society that produces an enduring and "normative" way of thinking that has dominated the world through White supremacy. It exists in our educational, economic, and justice systems. Systems have a way of spreading logic and offering benefits for accomplices in supporting the status quo—even if they are not at the center of power (e.g., people of color in a White dominant society).

Systemic analysis requires searching for and examining extreme examples of what is happening in society. We examine those extreme cases because they reflect the mainstream and give us greater insights into the social system. Whether it is a mass shooting in New Zealand, a march in Charlottesville, viral videos of Catholic school boys facing off with Indigenous protesters, a White CVS employee calling the police on a Black patron, or a White couple driving their six children off of a cliff in a murder-suicide—all of these play a role in our systemic analysis of what is happening in society, so that we can cultivate a critical consciousness as a means of working toward racial justice.

While we engage in this work, we constantly think about the question: Who is this book for? The target audience as we wrote the chapters and sought feedback from our peers was the metropolitan White liberal. In an aspirational way, we hope that White moderates will also read the book, and even a few White conservatives. In a deeper way, we hope that people of color will read this book to engage in the complexity of the ways in which White ideology is manifested outside of White bodies.

If classes, workshops, books, and organizations committed to racial justice center White people as the primary site of where the work needs to happen, then the project will fall short. Our colleague and co-author of *White Jesus*, Tabatha Jones Jolivet, often says, "Nothing about us, without us, is for us." It is a mantra used in the work of several movements (in her case Black Lives Matter), and in the case of this book, it highlight that White folks who need to "do their work" still cannot be left in isolation and to their own devices. If Whiteness evolved through cultivating anti-Blackness, the reconfiguration that has to take place, both individually and socially, is immense.

Furthermore, if collective solidarity is a prerequisite for effective work in social evolution, then the misguided notion that being on the cutting edge of all things diversity and justice only means focusing on individual oppression and pointing out the mistakes of other people, needs to change. Understanding individual oppression is essential, but without a commitment for everyone engaged in anti-racist justice work to be able to identify the ways in which they still need to grow—the project may fall short. Pointing out the mistakes and even stupidity of others often comes across as a quest for moral authority. In this way, the wrongness of another contributes to my expertise, which is a faulty way to build a logic system. Centering the need for White people to "do their work" in diversity spaces, oppression Olympics (the quest to be the most oppressed), and moral authority through the stupidity of others are all detrimental to the efforts of this book project on the struggle for racial consciousness.

That someone could claim offense (in a socially acceptable way) to a comment or an idea in a class room, board room, or office, actually began as a strategy to resist oppression. Then a broad application of claiming offense across a whole variety of social factors emerged, and watered down the strategy making it less effective for resisting oppression. Even worse, it allowed the power undergirding social conservatism to first criticize claiming offense as weakness (e.g., snowflakes) and then it later co-opted claims to offense. For example, the "oppression" faced by Trump-supporting conservatives. Now, claims to offense have been weaponized and used extensively on both sides of the power line. If everything is offensive, then the truly offensive issues get insulated from critical examination. In call out culture, all claims to offense become equal because of the sheer volume of the claims. What started as resistance to oppression has lost some effectiveness, which means that strategies also need to evolve.

Our doctoral students have brought us to the place of writing this work. In many ways, they have been our teachers. It is important to identify who we *think* the book is for, because it will give an indication of the mental audience that was present at the time of the writing. It is also important to note that we cannot be all-knowing with regard to who the book is for, and we hope that an unexpected audience will emerge as the book makes its way into spaces unknown to us.

We also want to note that we have attempted to write in a way that might produce thought and action. However, this is not a how-to book. It does not provide a list of items to do and to avoid. A persistent refrain that we notice in the media and in the critique of higher education is the perception of an overly mandated, politically correct, and inclusive language that both radical-izes and polices university students. It makes them, in a word, coddled.[5] Our daily context is higher education, and it is another indicator of how our soci-ety is developing. While colleges are often depicted as liberalizing forces, they have also been sites for new overt supremacist identity groups and movements like Evropa, Proud Boys, and It's OK to be White. Higher education is a site of identity development, struggle, and wrestling with new ways to sort out the complex social realities.

Just like its predecessors *White Out* and *White Jesus*, this book was born out of tension, agony, excavation, and longing. Over the past decade, we have taught doctoral courses, spoken at college campuses, both secular and sacred, around the globe, and conducted numerous workshops for faculty, staff, and students on issues related to diversity and racial justice in higher education. These books are the result of deep self-excavation and reflec-tion. We are in a constant state of examination of our own logic, in need of suspending our initial thoughts to explore other ideas, and we remind each other daily to cultivate our vulnerability, but not our fragility. We con-tinue to find new landscapes of cultural humility. Throughout most of our interactions, we have heard recurring objections, rebuttals, and arguments from students and colleagues at all levels within the academy. It was through these conversations that we sought to develop new language in an attempt to reshape well-established concepts. We undertook this task in order to articulate more clearly what we have heard, mostly from folks in the dominant White majority.

White Global South

For the last five years we have made annual visits to South Africa with doctoral students. Each year in South Africa, we visited Robben Island, which is known for the imprisonment of those accused of political crimes. Nelson Mandela was held there for 18 years (1964–1982) for working with the African National Congress against the oppressive White apartheid regime and the Nationalist Party. Each time we visited, a former political prisoner gave a tour of the prison. During one visit our guide asked me (Collins) to hold the key to Mandela's cell. I took a picture (Figure P.1) of my hand holding the key with a sense of symbolism and a reminder that a White hand turned the lock on that cell (and many others) thousands of times.

My consciousness of that oppressive regime and the role White supremacy played in that regime remains an essential part of my growth. Feeling guilt or seeking sympathy about my connection to the past and its role in the present will do little to cultivate a collective critical racial consciousness. Rather than stopping with White guilt or cultivating fragility, we have constructed a narrative about a systemic deconstruction of White supremacy.

During a 2019 visit, several of our hosts referred to Black conscientization. It came in reference to the importance of knowing and believing that a Black body and mind is inherently beautiful and profound (see more on Black consciousness from the slain anti-apartheid activist, Steve Biko). With conscientization comes the learning that you do not have to think White (i.e., excel in a White Western curriculum) or look White (i.e., straighten your hair and lighten your skin) in order to be valued. What might *racial consciousness* look like in a world where the White architecture of the mind has cemented the roads to privilege via the oppression of others?

Also imprisoned on Robben Island with Nelson Mandela was Robert Sobukwe. Arrested for his work with the Pan African Congress while he was a lecturer at the University of Witwatersrand;[6] his advocacy and activism led to rejecting the pass laws requiring the monitoring of people through carrying

Figure P.1: Key in Hand. The key to Nelson Mandela's jail cell on Robben Island, taken by author

a *dompas* (literally meaning dumb pass). For his activism he was sentenced to three years in prison, which turned into six years and he was released in 1969.

His belief that people across the African continent should unite together was an *idea* so threatening to the oppressive Nationalist Party, that they not only imprisoned him on the island, but they put him in his own building in solitary confinement and did not allow any contact with other prisoners. No one was allowed to speak to him for long periods of time. The isolation and imprisonment eroded his mind and left him psychologically damaged for a period of time.

He was eventually moved off the island for humanitarian reasons but died at the young age of 53. The level of psychological torture on Sobukwe was cruel and inhumane. During the six years he was in solitary confinement on

Robben Island, it became clear that he was being isolated psychologically so that his mind would decay. When visited by a member of parliament in 1965, she said, "I'm Helen Suzman. How are you, Mr. Sobukwe?" He replied: "I am forgetting how to speak."[7] The hostile environment, the torture, the rotten food, and the inability to contact others distorted his psychological functions. He was moved into a different facility shortly after Helen Suzman's visit. Sobukwe knew that the authorities were trying to destroy his mind and their mechanism to do so was through solitary confinement on Robben Island. That collective ideas and consciousness can be so threatening to a White supremacist regime is an indicator of the importance of cultivating a critical consciousness. That isolation can steal the mind is further an indicator that interdependence is necessary part of human survival.

During the same period, the University of Stellenbosch was host and home to the apartheid ideology and regime. In fact, a professor of applied psychology (and later sociology), was an architect and political champion of apartheid. Hendrik Verwoerd used the university as a place to cultivate supremacy based on the notion that keeping different races separate would enhance the ability for different races to be neighborly. Sobukwe and Verwoerd and their university associations and ideologies demonstrate the potential for colleges and universities to be progressive in raising consciousness or detrimental to humanity by cultivating supremacy. Ultimately the clash of ideologies led to decades of oppression and what will likely prove to be centuries of inequality. Verwoerd was an ideological leader for separation and Sobukwe was a leader for emancipation, unity, and consciousness. Verwoerd worked to pass and extend the Sobukwe clause in parliament which allowed the government to continuously extend his sentence for fear of galvanizing the public to action.

In 1949, a 21-year-old Sobukwe was President of the Student Representatives Council as a college student. He gave an address where he articulated the connection between consciousness and interdependence, and showed that race-based hate and a racial ecology were on opposite ends of the spectrum. He explained:

> World civilization will not become complete until the African has made his full contribution … I wish to make it clear again that we are anti-nobody. We are pro-Africa. We breathe, we dream, we live Africa: because Africa and humanity are inseparable … The future of the world lies with the oppressed and the Africans are the most oppressed people on earth … It is necessary for human progress that Africa be fully developed and only the African can do so.[8]

Sobukwe's early speech and his evolving philosophy rejected White paternalism while emphasizing Black self-regard, rejected colonialism while embracing social responsibility, and rejected being anti-White while being anti-White supremacy.

The politics of separation were defended by oppression and violence, not only in South Africa, but also in other parts of the world. In an effort to better understand the spread of supremacist ideologies from the White centers of Europe and North America to the Southern Hemisphere, we are working on a new book entitled, *White Diaspora: Universities and the Invasion of the Global South* with our colleague Christopher B. Newman. The project examines how notions of White supremacy were incubated in the Southern hemisphere, particularly in South Africa, Zimbabwe, New Zealand, Australia, and Brazil. We examine how notions of White supremacy were transported and incubated in spite of the White diaspora in each of these regions. The answer reveals much about the nature of global White supremacy.

While visiting Stellenbosch University in June 2019, HIV/AIDs activist Vuyiseka Dubula told our doctoral students that patriarchy is bad for men. She proceeded to explain how the culture of toxic masculinity causes men to view Sexually Transmitted Infections (STI) as a sign of weakness, thus many choose not to undergo testing or treatment for HIV/AIDS, which leads to high levels of death in men. In a similar yet different way, White supremacy is bad for White people and for all carriers of the residue of White supremacy. This systemically transmitted disease is depleting our ecosystem and eroding the ability to live with a collective critical racial consciousness. The most effective antidote for White supremacy is a collective, continuous commitment to *ubuntu* (a Zulu word referring to the interdependence of humanity) and a constantly evolving consciousness toward racial justice.

Influencers

We are indebted to the many colleagues who have dialogued with us, especially to our graduate students who have continuously pressed us to think more deeply about issues of systemic racism, power, privilege, and dominance.

In the midst of a never-ending flow of national events, tragedies, and tense dialogues surrounding race relations these past few years, we continue to feel provoked. In the midst of teaching class and conducting research, we watched students of color share deeply profound stories of pain and turmoil. The juxtaposition of these stories with the typical reactions of White students was striking: their responses could be described as ambivalent, silently resistant, or awkward entries into these conversations. Again, we felt committed. As we have been furiously writing from 2016–2020, during which the events kept pouring in, the curriculum kept getting rewritten, and we came to a point where we knew this would be unfinished business. We decided to cement our ever-evolving thoughts and processing into a final copy.

The work we have done has been immensely influenced by writers and thinkers from all over the world. We cite many of them throughout the book, but we list a few here in the preface, not only to give them credit, but to encourage our readers to embrace these authors as well. Tabatha Jones Jolivet and Allison Ash (our co-authors from *White Jesus*) have taught us extensively about what we do not know or understand and lead us down a path of humility and grace. Lori Patton Davis and Nolan Cabrera have written extensively on issues of Whiteness that form an empirical and sound backdrop to the work we present here. In the earlier stages of our career, we have been deeply transformed by the work of William Tierney, the late Robert Rhoads, Sylvia Hurtado, Mitch Chang, Darryl Smith, Estela Bensimon, and Walter Allen. From the earliest stages of our formation, we are deeply indebted to the work of those who came before us and taught us, like Frantz Fanon, Cornel West, Henry Louis Gates Jr., William Julius Wilson, Alan Paton, James Cone, Paolo Freire, and Ada Maria Isasi Diaz. We are also thankful for good friends and colleagues who are invested in this work in a way that goes way beyond our ability, including Julie Park, Samuel Museus, Frank Harris III, Kimberly Griffin, Darnell Cole, Tracy Lachica Buenavista, Liliana Graces, Victor Saenz, Ryiad Shanjahan, Kaiwipuni "Punihei" Lipe, and many others. We are indebted to Paige Britton who dedicated countless hours of careful reading and editing to our writing. The use of your gifts has made this book so much better. We offer our gratitude to or graduate students, Monica Johnson, Allan Mathew, Nathan Risdon, and Sherrene DeLong, who read early drafts of our work and offered helpful critiques.

Our thoughts are in a continuous phase of formation and in need of review, input, and challenge to be accessible to as many people as possible. Although it is incomplete and imperfect, we intend this analysis to be an act of devotion to something far beyond ourselves.

Notes

1. Bantum, Brian. *The Death of Race: Building a New Christianity in a Racial World.* Minneapolis: Fortress Press, 2016.
2. *PBS.* Accessed May 28, 2019. https://www.pbs.org/wgbh/frontline/film/class-divided/.
3. "The Racial Divide: Women of Color & White Women." *Red Table Talk.* Accessed May 28, 2019. https://www.facebook.com/redtabletalk/videos/343064719835818/.
4. Saad, Layla F. "Me and White Supremacy Workbook." Accessed March 30, 2019. http://laylafsaad.com/meandwhitesupremacy-workbook. This is a powerful journey for people to take and we highly recommend going through the steps of the workbook.
5. Haidt, Greg Lukianoff and Jonathan. "How Trigger Warnings Are Hurting Mental Health on Campus." *The Atlantic.* July 31, 2017. Accessed April 18, 2019. https://www.theatlantic.com/magazine/archive/2015/09/the-coddling-of-the-american-mind/399356/.
6. Pogrund, Benjamin. *Robert Sobukwe: How Can Man Die Better.* Johannesburg: Jonathan Ball Publishers, 2015.
7. Ibid, p. 261.
8. Ibid, p. 37.

· 1 ·

WHITE EVOLUTION AND THE WHITE ARCHITECTURE OF THE MIND

People communicate in contradictions. It is a hidden rhetorical device embedded in a typical phrase like, "Not to interrupt, but ...." The statement "Not to interrupt" is, in fact, an interruption. Likewise, the statement "Not to be rude, but ..." is typically followed by a rude statement. Such contradictions are intended to mitigate the offense of the action, but instead the contradictions mask the authenticity of both the intent and impact. Similarly, when a person says, "Not to be racist, but ..." what typically follows is a racially charged comment. The contradictory communication simultaneously conceals and betrays the intent.

Another contradiction that occurs along racial lines is the recurring charge of oversensitivity to race. As conversations about diversity have become central to the 24-hour news cycle, activism, and educational settings, the backlash against word policing, overreactions, trigger warnings, and similar conventions have characterized efforts at becoming more open and inclusive as *coddling* the weak and offering excessive attention to "snowflakes." Conservative advocates against word-policing have simultaneously labeled liberal thinkers "snowflakes" and put out an alert about liberal bias on college campuses (consider President Trump's executive order about free speech on campuses in March 2019).[1] What does it mean to criticize oversensitivity

Figure 1.1: Author's rendering of a roadside sign in Alabama

with terms like "snowflake" and "overreactive," while concurrently claiming that White conservatives are the most oppressed class of people? A roadside sign with a confederate flag in Alabama was posted on social media with the text in Figure 1.1, indicating that being White, straight, and conservative are essentially oppressed (as opposed to oppressor) identities, rather than the privileged.

Contradictions embedded in communication and ideology make it difficult to navigate the complexities of social relationships, especially regarding race. Throughout this book, we make a concerted effort to decode logic systems—that is, to understand the mental architecture on which they are built. Our purpose is to look at this architecture not as a static design, but as something in need of renovation and re-scripting. In order to introduce this topic, we examine the insidious efforts of engineering a pure White race through eugenics as a scientific attempt at supremacy, and then we recast the notion of White evolution in ecological terms of interdependence.

Engineering Evolution for Supremacy

The idea of a White race was formulated through a variety of components. Inferiority and slavery have existed alongside class and economic lines throughout human history; but in the eighteenth century, however, notions of freedom became associated with the adjective *White*. In 1790, U.S. citizens were defined as free White men. The added elements of pseudo-science, pigmentation, geography, cranium shape/size, and notions of beauty were combined to lay the architecture for *scientifically* constructing a White race.[2] The White race could not be fully defined without an articulation of what did not count as White, with a focus on dealing with social degenerates and the "feeble-minded." Thus, a variety of social behaviors were associated with race to cement the social construct. Nonracial markers of

Whiteness included income level, dress, education, cuisine, and a variety of other factors.

Biological and social conceptions of evolution are pathways for understanding the degree to which living beings and systems adapt to survive. Darwinian evolutionary biology is a pattern-based theory that demonstrates how plants and animals respond to stimuli and adapt accordingly. Social Darwinism is a more sinister lens which has been used to advocate that groups of people not performing well in society should be left to suffer without intervention. It is sinister precisely because the very conditions that led to the suffering were established through hierarchy, supremacy, and colorism. To take a socially constructed source of suffering and then interpret low quality of life as an *indicator* of a lack of survivability (as opposed to an indicator about the system that created the condition) is perverse and abusive. Social Darwinism is not a cohesive or uniform philosophy, but it is connected to eugenics—the "science" of trying to preserve desirable traits in genetics and procreation. The combination of social Darwinism, eugenics, and racism/colorism has been disastrous for humanity and a cornerstone of hierarchy and the evolution of dominance. In its historical context, White evolution has been profoundly supremacist and violent.

Modern science and a form of democracy grew out of a period of history called the *Enlightenment*, when people professed to relentlessly pursue the truth even if it meant rejecting tradition. During this same period, the foundation for understanding difference, discrimination, slavery, and supremacy gained momentum. Thomas Jefferson, author of the famous words, "We hold these truths to be self-evident, that all men are created equal," had conflicted notions of what counted as "truth," "human," and "equal," despite his confident contributions to writing the Declaration of Independence. He encouraged "scientific investigations" into those notions and incorporated them in the development of law. In 1781 he wrote, "Why not retain and incorporate the blacks into the state?" and added, "The blacks, whether originally a distinct race, or made distinct by time and circumstances are inferior to whites in the endowments both of body and mind."[3]

Jefferson's racial conceptions of Black and White provide a lens for understanding Enlightenment thinking and the architecture of founding ideologies for the United States. Furthermore, the fact that Jefferson owned and enslaved other human beings and conceived children with Sally Hemings, whom his wife inherited, drives the analysis a step further. In 2017, a secret room in his house was discovered where he likely kept Sally and the multiple children he fathered. Though no one else was in the room when it happened, his private actions provide public insights demonstrating his writings are in fact slavery documents, and that his assertions of liberty and freedom were limited by conceptions of White supremacy.

The Enlightenment was an exercise in the social construction of inferiority under the guise of the pursuit of truth, occurring in the name of science and under the veneer of objectivity. Throughout the early to mid-1800s, the top medical scientists in the world were using *phrenology*, the study of craniums, to determine connections between intelligence and race, as their work contributed to advancing notions of inferiority rooted in evolutionary science. Over a short period of time, *scientific knowledge* became *conventional wisdom*, which then shaped social structures, including laws, education, economics, and property ownership. During this time, Darwin was writing observations and theories about the needs for survival and the characteristics of species that survive and adapt compared to those that do not. Later in the nineteenth century, Darwin's cousin began a movement, centered around eugenics, to propagate the British elite. It did not gain much momentum in England, but did in the United States. The notion of social Darwinism and eugenics spread throughout universities and upper-class society as a means of confirming their survival as the fittest, as well as strategizing about how to weed out their inferiors.[4]

Social constructions are sometimes thought to be too abstract or, more pessimistically, a conspiracy-oriented lens through which to view society. A close look at history, however, dispels the abstract and reveals the tragic architecture on which society is built. Consider the culmination of science, progress, liberal society, and democracy in a post-slavery Reconstruction state. All of these concepts came together in a eugenics movement that was cemented in a Supreme Court case (*Buck v. Bell*, 1927), which reinforced laws that permitted sterilizing the "feeble-minded" (i.e., poor and racially minoritized women), and which was not overturned until the late twentieth century.[5] *Feeble-minded* was a legal construct that allowed the government to exterminate the ability of women to sexually reproduce, based on an ideologically driven masquerade of objective science and claims about human progress (see Figure 1.2[6]).

In 2018, Alice Minium wrote that sterilization and eugenics "were a means to medically re-engineer society in the image of white masculinity," which she labeled a period of "Progressive Genocide."[7] It was social construction with the *best of intentions* to help humanity progress. After all, a state-run home

Figure 1.2: Eugenics: Roots and fruits available from Wikimedia commons in the public domain

for the feeble-minded was built in Virginia as a place to house people whose parents were not able to reproduce socially desirable offspring. The United States was the first country to legalize these actions and paved the way for Nazi-regime social engineering in Germany. Many states participated. Tens of thousands of women were sterilized against their knowledge and/or will. This continued for many years, though it took different forms in different states. The Virginia Sterilization Act, for example, was not overturned until 1972.

Consider the example of civil rights activist Fannie Lou Hamer, who entered a hospital in Mississippi in 1961 to have a tumor removed. The doctor had the authority to diagnose her as feeble-minded, and he proceeded to give her a hysterectomy without her knowledge or consent. They were able to do this under compulsory sterilization laws designed to reduce the number of people with undesirable traits. Fannie Lou Hamer was credited with coining the expression "Mississippi Appendectomy," after this involuntary sterilization.[8]

Even prior to that event, investigative journalist and civil rights activist Ida B. Wells compiled evidence to show that lynching often occurred in
an effort punish people of color and to protect White women—the keep-
ers of the ability to procreate desirable traits.[9] Lynching was seen as a necessary method of precaution, a means to safeguard the carriers of the White
race (i.e., White women). This is a profound collision of science, violence,
hierarchy, and White supremacy. Records of lynching justifications centered
around perceived or constructed threats of raping White women. Even the
infamous movie *Birth of a Nation* portrays the scene of a Black man pursuing
a White woman. Fear was used to justify violence in defense of preserving the
purity of the race and the White women who can deliver that purity. Through
defining inferiority via feeble-mindedness, color, and economic status, the law
also implicitly defined *superiority*. The logic used to establish these social constructs is still detectable in contemporary rhetoric.

History is replete with many extensive examples of the ways in which
these connections served to use *scientific thought* in service of White supremacy. Enslavement and anti-Blackness play a primary historical and contextual
role, but Congress also connected ethnicity, race, and nationality in the 1882
Chinese Exclusion Act. The act was rooted in an argument about maintaining public health. Only twenty years prior, a physician wrote a report entitled "Chinese Immigration and the Physiological Causes of the Decay of a
Nation."[10] Part one of the report explains the supremacy of intellect and beauty
found in the "Caucasian" race and the divine appointment of that supremacy.
Part two of the report details threats to health like syphilis, mental alienation, and tobacco. The solution was clear—preserve the race. This report
inspired the California Board of Health to investigate the potential harm of
intermixing races to public health, and two decades later this type of thinking
produced a federal act of historic proportions. In 1875, Chinese women were
banned from immigrating to the U.S. under the Page Act. Thus, the White
evolution of superiority included a systematic and structural approach to using
people of other races as labor, while at the same time using the law to prevent
any potential threats to the country's racial purity.

The impact of racial trauma and systemic injustice lasts for centuries.
Recent studies of epigenetics suggest trauma may have such a deep influence
that it alters DNA.[11] For example, exploratory studies on the DNA of holocaust survivors and their descendants showed some indicators that the violence in concentration camps *altered* part of the genetic code that was passed
on to descendants. Other studies have been conducted on victims of famine,

war, and trauma that make connections between the role of damage and the way in which it is passed on, not only in memory, but in actual genetics. We are walking a precarious line by bringing in epigenetics while criticizing eugenics. Genetic attributions to someone's worth, ability, and even health as it relates to race are inherently dangerous. Our purpose here is to highlight the ongoing ecological harm stemming from oppression, violence, and supremacy.

If epigenetics shows that there is even a *possibility* that social experiences can alter our biological nature, it brings another layer of depth to the role of racial violence from slavery to lynching. If trauma shows some indication of prompting genetic alteration, what might that imply for the oppressor? If having supremacist oppressor ancestors could have altered your DNA, it would certainly change the conversation around what was in the past versus the present. In the book *Knowledge in the Blood*, Jonathan Jansen explores a post-apartheid South Africa where White college students perpetuate a racist history that they never actually experienced.[12] The notion of "knowledge in the blood" is an exploration of how society and people groups reproduce ideology. There may be as much of a genetic element as the social, but the two were already combined through efforts like phrenology and eugenics. We continue to extend the question, if trauma can alter DNA, what might happen to the DNA of the one who inflicted the trauma? The intensity of socializing White dominant oppressors may have deep implications for future generations. Consequently, when White people use the excuse, "I did not own slaves," or "That was a long time ago," we can speculate to the contrary that the biological and social implications of our ancestors' actions do in fact weigh heavily on our contemporary social systems and in the physical bodies we occupy.

To be clear, we are not making a "scientific" argument about race. Instead we are demonstrating how science and race have been powerfully fused to perpetuate supremacy. Supremacy is mutating and showing up in new and disturbing ways. *The Bell Curve* by Richard Herrnstein and Charles Murray was just one deplorable example in a long history. Every year, articles are published in academic journals using race as some factor in explaining intelligence. Nicholas Wade, a journalist and editorial writer about science, published a book entitled *A Troublesome Inheritance* to explain connections between genetic evolution and race. Though the arguments are nuanced, the outcome is predictable—the White race gets a roundabout genetic accolade for its superior disposition. In the preface to the second edition, Wade responds to the many critiques of the book and goes to great lengths to explain that his argument is not racist and cannot be used to support racism. It is a more sophisticated introduction than simply stating, "Not to be racist, but...".

Science is not objective, culturally detached, or an omniscient lens through which to view the world. Science, as it is generally used, is an appendage of the White Western logic system that dominates a market-driven and hierarchical world. The diversity of knowledge that has been passed down through cultures all over the world has been relegated as storytelling or cosmology by the Western knowledge system known as science—and that is racist. Our purpose here is to twist the idea of evolution and apply it to a collective critical racial consciousness by using an ecosystems analogy. Even as we use the idea of evolution as metaphor, a critically spirited reader will invariably find gaps in our analogies and then begin to question our approach as a means to invalidate and cancel us, but we underscore how we are not making a scientific argument.

The history of how White supremacy was constructed and articulated through "rigorous science" is both deep and wide. In the construction of superiority, the Goddard-Binet test (later the Stanford-Binet test) became a way to "objectively measure" feeble-mindedness, which identified those who needed to be isolated, alienated, or removed from society. These tests are the very basis of the modern Intelligence Quotient (IQ) and standardized tests for college entrance exams. In 1933 Nazi Germany embraced the U.S. version of eugenics and adapted the rhetoric of weeding out faulty or bad genetics as a matter of public health and human survival.[13] In the case of Nazi Germany, the perceived threat to humanity was people of Jewish descent. Although Nazi Germany's adaptation of eugenics is almost universally regarded as "evil," the liberal-minded state of California was itself an epicenter of eugenics in the 1930s. Bankers, members of the University of California regents, and the Stanford University president were all supportive of eugenics.[14] In 1934, California hosted an exhibit to display the success of the science and to show how influential the state had been on the German adoption of eugenics.

These profound illustrations of the ways in which White evolution was comprehensively constructed as a violent path to supremacy are only a handful of the examples available. We chose these selections as a foundation to demonstrate the concrete path to the architecture of both inferiority and superiority, in order to forge a new path to negate the old architecture. As noted by Frantz Fanon, "[T]he juxtaposition of the black and white races has resulted in a massive psycho-existential complex"; and, in the same vein as Fanon, "By analyzing it we aim to destroy it."[15] It is impossible to emerge or evolve into a different kind of racial trajectory without being immersed in and understanding the vast influence of White supremacy on science, economics, law, education, and religion. The faulty logics on which the mind has been built must be decoded to be understood, and deconstructed before reconstructed.

White Evolution and an Ecology of Racial Justice

Taking stock of the plethora of milestones in the historical evolution of supremacy, we offer propositions for a cognitive, epistemological, and spiritual revolution *against* supremacy. Can there be a White evolution that moves away from uniformity, or racial purity, as a cornerstone of supremacy and survival, to *diversity and interdependence* as a necessary construct for survival? If so, the neurocognitive rewiring to evolve toward a racial awareness is immense and the struggle will be constant. We recognize the great distance between the current state of White supremacy and the potential for a new version of White evolution. Freire wrote, "I cannot think *for others* or *without others*," which we take to indicate a profound interconnectedness in the fabric of humanity.[16] Eugenics and the social evolution of uniformity as a principle recreates a monoculture through violence against the body.

When understood at the epistemological and social level, one potential effect of a monoculture is akin to the outcomes of inbreeding. By way of analogy, the biological effect of inbreeding is reduced cognitive function, reduced genetic diversity, reduced immune function, and increased risk of genetic orders. The negative consequences make our engagement with the metaphor of evolution apt in advocating for a diverse ecosystem rather than racial purity, monoculture, and hegemony. Instead of evolution being leveraged to *eradicate* competing definitions of reality and maintaining supremacy, we propose an evolution of the mind that is predicated on the belief that survival is an *interdependent* proposition. White evolution for racial consciousness requires a new embodiment and life of the mind that begins with a recognition of the following principles:

1. Systems of power in society replicate inequality based on differences in race, gender, sexuality, ability, etc.
2. A mutual benefit exists whereby individual actions, behaviors, and ideologies need to be affirmed by a system, and they in turn perpetuate that system of supremacy.

3. Systems that perpetuate supremacy must be deconstructed and replaced with an ecosystem that relies on a deep interdependence for epistemological, physical, and spiritual survival.
4. There is no arrival point to being woke. White supremacy has a tenacious ability to regenerate and reappear in new ways, both individually and systemically. As a result, the work of eradicating such systems is *never* finished.

The last point here is not fatalistic, though we understand that working without a finish line can cripple motivation. The purpose of the reminder that we are working for something that will never be complete, is to prevent a belief that inclinations toward White supremacy can be quickly outmaneuvered or overcome. For example, Eric Kaufman in the book *Whiteshift* addresses the future of White majorities, White identity, and White ethnicity. But even Kaufman addresses the question of demographics by treating White as something that is fixed. The fundamental shift in Whiteness, however, also includes the evolution of who is *included* as White. For example, the history of how Irish and Italian immigrants became White maps a path from being excluded from the White label to being included (see works by David Roediger). European Jews, who once were the object of severe European White aggression, now occupy a White status in many places around the globe. Under the apartheid era in South Africa, people could change or reclassify their race with the government. In 1985, 702 colored people, one Indian, and three Chinese became reclassified as White.[17] Addressing the browning of the globe is difficult, because those shifts may actually be new conditions for defining who else gets included as White. One condition for achieving White status in the past was power collusion in a commitment to global anti-Blackness.

For some, not having a final destination for racial awareness equates to never being good enough. Paradoxically, the acknowledgment that there is no end point cultivates greater potential for systemic change. It is part of consciousness. This set of requirements moves the notion of evolution away from a competition-based perspective, where one race or color survives to the detriment of another. Instead, this set of requirements determines survival based on the well-being of the whole. It is not a simplistic or easy proposition. It involves a deep understanding of the way mental architectures directs individuals to participate in systemic injustice, as well as a deep commitment to deconstructing that architecture on a regular basis. Because we believe that privilege and dominance is an evolving virus (see more in Chapter 3), our cognition and commitment to racial justice must also evolve at a clip that outpaces the predisposition for participation in supremacy.

The purpose here is to cultivate our human relationships and systems through a recognition of interdependence, in order to facilitate racial justice. Racial justice is equitable participation in all segments of society, with special attention to race. Justice is a large concept and a project that requires human agency to work interdependently toward change. Racial justice, then, is one component of the larger project, and it requires those in dominant positions of power to recognize their own complicity in a dynamic system that distributes resources and benefits unequally along racial lines. Racial justice is also a complex web because it includes cognitive justice, which is the recognition of the epistemic diversity in all societies and the recognition that there is no complete knowledge.[18] Supremacy is connected to hegemony, the idea that knowledge has only come from one people group. The belief that Western thought is the highest form of knowledge is cognitive supremacy and oppression. It led to a belief in objective science which also constructed anything outside of the scientific canon as either ignorant or mythology.

What we are proposing in terms of a White evolution and the struggle for racial consciousness is an incomplete proposition. Paradoxically, it is at times incompatible with some of the scholarship that influences the way we think about the topic of race. A tenet of Critical Race Theory is that the dominant group gets involved only upon receiving some type of benefit—the term is *interest convergence*. In this way, trying to understand a social construct (race) with biological comparisons can create some tension. Our intention to use evolution and ecology in a positive way is in tension with interest convergence. Continuing the biological illustration, there are at least three types of symbiotic relationships. The first is *parasitic*, where one organism feeds off of the other, which may be most like interest convergence. The second is *commensalism*, where one benefits, but the other is not harmed. Finally, in *mutualism* both partners benefit—and this is the type of interdependence we are trying to cultivate.

To understand and explore this justice-oriented White evolution, we return to concepts that were previously presented in the book *White Out* to revise, expand, and operationalize the study of Whiteness for the purpose of dismantling racist tendencies in individuals and racist structures in our institutions and society. We toggle back and forth between individual and systemic roles because they are interwoven in the process of reproducing power. "White out" is an umbrella term we introduced to cover a variety of strategies used to defend dominance. The White architecture of the mind is a concept that includes individual responses within systems that promote inequality and dominance. In another book, *White Jesus: The Architecture of Racism in Religion and Education*, we explored the religious participation in spiritual violence that championed Whiteness as a salvific harbinger of dominance. We expanded the notion of the White architecture of the mind to the White architecture of salvation, which is essentially the same logic system rooted in power and dominance but cloaked with divine authority. White evolution requires a decoding and deconstructing of each of these architectures in order to reconstruct a design for racial justice.

We have often told groups of White people that Whiteness is not about your individual guilt so much as it is about the ability of a system to create a hierarchy of privilege. Sometimes the attention to guilt (and the cathartic alleviation of guilt) makes the systemic level hard to see. In addition, this is not just about White people. Explicit and viral examples of White racist actions that are divorced from the systemic injustices in society—which can manifest in bodies of all colors—serve as a distraction from the ways in which anyone can be complicit in reinforcing injustice. The belief that the President or a White nationalist terrorist *is* the problem (as opposed to merely being *representative* of the problem) is a comfortable distraction. Obsessions with political correctness, politics, and evil caricatures obfuscate the reality of White supremacy and its tenacious adaptability. We heard Cornel West once say he is trying to "kill the White supremacist" that lives in him. This quote represents a concrete effort to evolve toward racial justice for both people of color and White people alike. Furthermore, the historical and social development of what counts as White involves not only skin tone (proportion of melanin), but disposition against Blackness. Historically, the spectrum of color came to represent non-color markers of Whiteness, which include professionalism, wealth, language, dress, patriarchy, and other codes to signal a place in society.

The White architectures of salvation and of the mind are adversarial logic systems rooted in power and colorism. They present seemingly objective principles, rules, and norms. In the religious sense they are codified and protected by a sacred canopy—socially constructed ideas presented with a *divine* authority (see Peter Berger). The benefits and costs of these architectures are realized in the fruits of segregated groups of people who throughout history have managed to leverage land, knowledge, education, economics, laws, social relationships, and natural resources to reinforce dominance and supremacy. Mottos (perhaps platitudes) like *In God We Trust* or *God First* cannot convey the character or commitments of an institution or superordinate identity. The statements may convey *In Our Version of God You Must Trust*, or *Our Variety of God First*. Statements about submitting to the will of a god are often rhetorical devices intended to communicate divine justification of human social constructions.

Logic systems and architectures are often difficult to see. Without any additional resources, try to predict the next line in the sequence below:

1

11

21

1211

111221

312211

13112221

This is a sequence that is often very difficult to ascertain at first glance. The riddle is called a Morris number sequence, and the logic is revealed in its informal name: look-and-say sequence. We have presented this sequence to advanced doctoral students in a class exercise, and they spent a fair amount of time trying to predict what string of numbers might come next. Rarely does a group come to recognize that each line is determined by reading aloud the line that precedes it. The first line, "1," determines the second line by reading aloud, "One, one." The answer, the next line in the sequence is: 1113213211. Without knowing the system, the rules of the game, the unspoken norms of society, individual actors are distributed and tracked by a mechanistic power system. However, with the recognition of a logic or architecture, it is easy to quickly determine the sequence, to know what comes next, and then to figure out how to re-wire, reconstruct, or evolve the system in a particular direction—in the case of this book, either toward supremacy or toward racial justice.

Colleges and universities—sites of knowledge production and diffusion—were central participants to the eugenics version of White evolution. There were dozens of universities that not only produced the leading thinkers in eugenics, but also provided labs and centers to promote the ideology, and hundreds of courses taken by thousands of students. The same is true for sterilization and other deeply flawed and violent ways of thinking. Because of their complicity in the original version of White evolution, as higher education professors we advocate that the very institutions that created and disseminated these ideas be more committed to anti-racism and justice. In order to disrupt the stealth modes of supremacy rooted in curricula and ideologies, this miseducation must be exposed and a commitment to racial justice must be a system-wide project.

Whiting Out

In the book *White Out*, we opened with a story about a doctoral student at a university in the southern half of the U.S. who was set to be one of the first Black graduates of his PhD program. He often outperformed his peers in academic achievements and was given honors for his efforts on completing his doctoral examinations. However, on one occasion after writing an exam in a standard blue book, his advisor responded to one answer in red ink with the comment, "N[word] you know better. This is to show you that race had nothing to do with your grade." The student went on to perform at the top level of the program and upon graduation his advisor claimed his role in the success of the first Black graduate of the program. The student built a successful career, but always kept that exam. In some ways, the comment attacked his mind and sense of self, and in other ways it motivated him.

One day, the newly minted PhD used Wite-Out, the name brand correction liquid, to cover up the comment, but left the blue book in his desk drawer. A few years later, students and fellow professors challenged the veteran professor for being insensitive and even racist. The professor went to see his former student to talk to him about these attacks and look for support and testimony that he was not a racist. The former student listened and then pulled out the old exam written in the blue book. He showed the professor the incendiary comment written years earlier, but the professor could not see it—the Wite-Out had covered up the comment. Because the professor could not see it through the Wite-Out, the student turned to all of the consecutive pages to show him the words that could be seen and felt because of the indentation. In spite of an attempt to blot out the words written in the blue book and the effect on his life, the indention went deep into the pages, and perhaps into the psyche of the lives of students subjected to this kind of interaction.

The vignette represents the concept of White Out—a strategy or set of habits that defend White dominance. It is the notion that attempts to cover systems, dispositions, and actions cannot cover their full indentation or impact. White Out, an action of intentional or unintentional blotting, obscures others' experiences in favor of a competing reality. The degree to which an experience can be denied creates space for a dominant conception to be defined as reality.[19] Actions and experiences combine to create and perpetuate a particular reality; and as competition increases and threats to power emerge, new realities evolve. Colorism and White dominance are fixtures in contemporary reality. The evolution of society includes new hierarchies and new forms of dominance.

Social Construction

This book is also about the dominant role of Whiteness in a racially diverse society. Whiteness is a socially constructed status that is sometimes assumed to be biological, since it relates to skin color. Race is undoubtedly a social construct, as various periods in history show that Whiteness was an achievable status. Again, consider the early Italian and Irish immigrants to the United States and their ability to achieve a legal White status, while Africans who were forced to immigrate under slavery were denied privileges and assigned the status of property.[20] The social construction of race has manifested in similar ways throughout history. As alluded to earlier, the category of being *colored* in South Africa has a specific history of colonists and natives intermingling and moving to the interior of the region. In Trevor Noah's book, *Born a Crime*, he explains the ways in which those considered colored or even light skinned are essentially offered a path to being White—as long as they do not mess up where they live, go to school, and marry—all of which are signals of Whiteness. Social constructionism provides a method for decoding societal logic. Ideas become habits, then routines, then legitimized knowledge, and ultimately a socially constructed reality. Threats to the reality (or status quo) must either be assimilated or annihilated (see the previous section on eugenics).

We define Whiteness as a system. Much has been said about the psycho-social attitudes about race, and although we address those, we are predominantly concerned with a larger system that has constructed such a dominant reality that it narrows our sense of choices and beliefs relating to race. The interactions between systems and individuals helps to give insights into how systems are built, sustained, and maintained through individual and group actions. The systems in which we live and operate can be compared to architecture, or a design that creates limited choices one can make when it comes to moving into certain spaces, opening doors, staying, or departing.

Consider the fable of the giraffe and the elephant.[21] A giraffe is the cornerstone of the fable, and he has just finished building a house. It was a perfect house for his family's needs. It had high windows, which allowed for privacy and lots of light. It had narrow hallways, which allowed for maximum use of space in a convenient passageway. This perfectly designed house was the pride of the neighborhood and won national awards for its design. While the giraffe was working in his shop one day, he looked out the window and saw an elephant he knew who was also a woodworker. Much to the delight of the elephant, the giraffe invited him in to see the woodshop. After small-talk, they encountered a problem—the elephant could only get his head through the doorway. The giraffe noted that this was not a serious problem, however, because extra doors had been designed to accommodate his woodshop equipment; and so, the elephant ultimately was able to get inside.

While they were chatting about woodworking, the giraffe's wife called from upstairs to tell the giraffe he needed to talk to his supervisor on the phone. The giraffe told the elephant he had to go upstairs and that it might take a while, so to make himself at home. After some time, the elephant thought he'd better go upstairs to see what was happening—and ended up causing terrible damage to the stairs, the walls, and the décor. The giraffe ran to see the commotion and asked what the elephant was doing; the elephant answered that he was just "making himself at home." The giraffe suggested that if he took some aerobic classes, he might be able to slim down and fit through the passageways and not cause so much damage to the stairs. The elephant responded that a house designed for a giraffe might never work for an elephant.

Here is where the original parable ends. While the story serves to demonstrate unintentional racial injustice, there are many ways to advance other streams of thought from the original idea in the story. In fact, one could imagine a simple fix by flipping the script: that is, to see elephants slowly moving into the homes and communities once occupied by giraffes. One could assume that giraffes migrated in a large group to a newer suburban community in a movement of *giraffe flight*—nothing against elephants, of course, but they felt the neighborhood was changing for the worse. So even as elephants become the compositional majority group in that community, the dominant factors that favored giraffes remain intact. The curricula in the local schools may still be of giraffe history, for example, and the traditions within the neighborhood are still largely remnants of a giraffe frame of mind.

Perhaps some elephants themselves have embodied a dominant giraffe frame of mind, and have associated success in the world as tantamount to a casting off of their own elephant culture, going so far as to change their appearance (through plastic surgery and cosmetics), mannerisms, language, behavior and hobbies to assimilate into a dominant giraffe culture. Some assimilated elephants might go so far as to offer advice to other less refined elephants regarding the keys to their success. The result is a sense of self-hate and internalized oppression for the elephants, who were expected to excel in a society never meant for them.

The simple story of the giraffe and elephant is a basic way to demonstrate the skeleton structure of our own society. And just like the elephants, a kind of self-hate begins to take root within the souls of people of color, and oftentimes their own cultural identity and appreciation become extinct. Upon realizing this, they mourn the loss of their unique identities that have been eviscerated and can never be retrieved.

The recognizable application to diverse groups of people occupying the same space conveys that much of reality (or architecture) is designed to be the best fit for one group. Because it is a dominant reality, any group for whom the architecture does not work is blamed for the lack of fit; that is, being estranged is the fault of the persons in that group—an individual problem that could be adjusted merely by assimilating. From our perspective, the giraffe's house represents the systemic Whiteness that permeates the United States and even the larger global sense of reality. Of course, fables and analogies fail to represent the full complexity of the subject matter. For example, the giraffe and elephant story does not capture the long history between giraffes and elephants, the disparate generational sources of wealth, and the ongoing denial of any difference in a post-civil rights era. The issue goes much deeper than physical space or even policy environments, and into the White architecture of the mind. Similar to physical architecture that restricts and guides action, the available choices individuals are able to make, and the degree to which groups can interact, the White architecture of the mind restricts and guides choices, reactions, and responses.

Implicit Bias

One aspect of analyzing mental architecture involves recognizing where thinking occurs as either fast or slow.[22] "Thinking fast" is another way of describing automatic and reactionary thoughts. For example, when reading the problem 2+2, it is virtually impossible to avoid generating the answer. However, when reading the problem 14×37, additional labor may be required to generate the answer. Even if given multiple-choice options, the answer may not be immediately discernible indicating that one must think more slowly to generate the right choice.

In the Muller-Lyer illusion reproduced in Figure 1.3, two parallel lines are shown, with the question of which is longer.[23]

Typically, the human eye and brain connection interprets the illusion so that the bottom line, with arrows pointing out, appears shorter than the top line. Fixed measurement, however, shows the lines to be the exact same length, in spite of this typical visual-mental response. However, upon seeing the illusion for the second time, even if it looks like the bottom line is shorter, when asked the question, people will respond that the lines are the same length. This is a neurocognitive rewiring of the brain—a new space in the mental architecture to respond to tricks or illusions. In one exercise, we use an alternate version of the illusion where the bottom line is in fact shorter to see how students respond. Participants typically indicate that they are the same length, which highlights how *thinking slow* becomes *thinking fast* and leaves later responses vulnerable to similar mistakes.

Applications of thinking fast or reacting automatically in diverse groups of people are related to the notion of implicit bias. Project Implicit, based at Harvard University, offers the Implicit Association Test (IAT). The Project claims that the test measures attitudes and beliefs that people may be unwilling or unable to report. The IAT may be especially interesting if it shows that one has an implicit attitude, which was previously unacknowledged. For example, one may believe that women and men should be equally associated with science, but when automatic associations demonstrate that a person

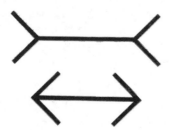

Figure 1.3: Muller-Lyer Illusion

associates men with science more than women, the tool serves to highlight a place in the mind that need to be reconstructed.[24]

The test uses fast thinking to uncover embedded or implicit value constructs about a variety of identities. The test filters implicit thinking by examining strength of associations between concepts (e.g., black people, gay people) and evaluations (e.g., good, bad) or stereotypes (e.g., athletic, clumsy). Responses come more quickly or easily when closely related items share the same response key. In the 1940s, Clark and Clark conducted the famous doll study which revealed that both White and Black children showed preferences for lighter skin.[25] The study was used to support arguments in the *Brown v. Board of Education* case about segregation, and it was recreated on a small scale by child psychologist and University of Chicago professor Margaret Beale Spencer in 2010. Spencer's study found that White children have a high rate of White bias and that Black children also have White bias, though at a lower rate. Spencer also found that racial attitudes do not evolve as children grow older.[26] Thinking slow (or intentionally with effort) provides an opportunity to rewire automatic responses, which is required to compete with the implicit or unconscious mental architecture that guides decision-making.

The White architecture of the mind is a term and an analogy to highlight that the mind is a result of a set of blueprints, constructions, walls, doors, windows, and pathways that influence and predispose individuals to react based on a systemic logic that was socially constructed. Put differently, we use the term to indicate the *individual* actions, choices, behaviors, and attitudes that are guided by a *socially* constructed system that predisposes these attitudes and grants privileges and accessibilities to core members of a dominant group. Frantz Fanon explained White fear of Blackness in this way: "[T]he body of the black man hinders the closure of the white man's postural schema at the very moment when the black man emerges into the white man's phenomenal world."[27] For example, if someone chooses a house in a gated neighborhood with a particular style and level of prestige, it may be reasonable to think it was all a matter of individual choice and fit. However, there was a system of priming effects that conditioned the individual to be attracted to a particular style and a system of builders, city codes, and Home Owners Association regulations that led to the creation of the neighborhood, in addition to the segmented way populations group together based on race and income. That system and all of its components create an architecture of the mind, and when it goes unrecognized, decisions are thought to be purely of individual volition exercised by the rational mind alone.

Similar to the ongoing nurture vs. nature debate in the social and natural sciences, there is an individual vs. systemic debate in the quest for explaining society's largely disparate outcomes when it comes to income, wealth, education, standardized test scores, employment, and crime rates, all of which are divided along racial lines. Is it a matter of individuals needing to make choices, or is society directed by a social construction built upon White privilege? But the individual is a producer of society, and society a producer of the individual. Linking back to the discussion of eugenics and the engineering of a pure race, the White family is guardian of that structure. As "society is the sum of all the families," so is the White family the "educating and training ground for entry into society."[28]

Take, for example, a White person engaging in direct social action to combat racism. Imagine this person to be familiar with intercultural terminology and to be well educated. Privilege may be acknowledged, but not racism, as that is often assumed to be an individual attitude and corresponding set of actions. Trying to understand the deeply embedded impact of racism becomes difficult in the case of such an individual because his or her overt actions are not racist and it can be difficult to observe someone's underlying racist beliefs. As a result, bell hooks shifted the means to understand pervasively oppressive social structures from racism to White supremacy. She wrote,

> When liberal whites fail to understand how they can and/or do embody white supremacist values and beliefs even though they may not embrace racism ... they cannot recognize the ways their actions support and affirm the very structure or racist domination and oppression that they wish to see eradicated.[29]

By using hooks' notion of White supremacy, we also try to focus on how a White architecture is essential to defending and dismantling White dominance.

Dominance beyond Whiteness

When we presented this framework to a group of colleagues, a White female was the first to ask a question: "Do you distinguish between White males and females?" It was an appropriate first question, given the complexity of multidimensional intersectionality embedded within a socially constructed reality.[30] The question points back to the root of social arrangements concerning power, where dominance is also coupled with being male, cisgender, straight, a U.S. citizen, middle or upper class, and many other salient identities. Some of these realities around class, gender, and sexuality serve as markers and indicators of Whiteness or the path to Whiteness (consider the role of class and skin tone in Indian caste systems or in Southeast Asia). We acknowledge and identify the importance of these constructed power arrangements and the additional complexity that comes with intersections.

We believe that race is not a singular dimension but rather embodies the social complexity of multiple discriminatory barriers. Race was amalgamated over time as a proxy for factors ranging from religion, geography, class, property, and scientific classification. Social life should be analyzed through the complexity of multiple factors of dominance and oppression, and in this book we look at the ways in which race is an intersectional composite and proxy for superiority. Though the intersectional lens has been misused in a variety of ways (see more from Patricia Hill Collins and Sirma Bilge in their book, *Intersectionality*), we examine how one of the strongest defenses of White dominance is a deflection of Whiteness onto some other status that is used to mitigate the benefit associated with being White. This particular point is salient to Chapter 3, which explores the tragic story of the Hart family.

We ask the reader to consider your own positionality in relation to social realities. Intersecting identities and being multi-contextual is a fixed aspect of many folks who live and have lived in the reality of "double consciousness," as coined by W. E. B. Du Bois;[31] but it is also the multiple consciousness of people of color, women, queer folks, and others who do not have the privilege of functioning in the single reality driven by White dominance. As authors of the book, our consciousness demands a vision of multiple realities; and we advocate for an expanding consciousness through decolonization, because we are both subject to internalizing Whiteness and other forms of dominance (even though only one of us is White). The perpetuation of White dominance is not simply about individual White identity, but is a project in which minoritized peoples play a role. Internalized oppression can reinforce the White architecture of the mind—a critical link between oppressive systems and individual actors in the system.

Many of the examples we give, and our own reflections, are rooted in a Black-White binary. Similar to other issues of intersectionality, we do not intend for this to be the whole of the conversation. I (Collins) am White and I (Jun) am Korean-American. We find that the Black-White binary is an important starting point for understanding the dominance of White systems and how they are perpetuated, but it is certainly not the end of the discussion. Furthermore, we have found that White supremacy and anti-Blackness are global trends. When we say Black and/or White we are neither being dichotomous nor exclusively talking about individuals essentialized as White or Black. Instead we are addressing global anti-Blackness, a framework created by a White social structure.

There is a continuum of race and color, but giving examples in Black and White does not exclude someone who is Latinx or Asian. Whether in South Africa (see Trevor Noah), France (see Frantz Fanon), Australia, or the United States (see David Roediger), there has always been a path to achieving Whiteness—a verification of the social construction of superiority depicted through color/race. Similarly, there is also a social construct of Black (and it is not always "from African descent"—see, e.g. aboriginals in Australia)— all of which is the ultimate verification of the social construction of inferiority, depicted through color/race. The irony, of course, is that all of this moves from a construction of inferiority versus superiority to an essentialized identity. A person learns to think, "I am White, therefore superior," and vice versa. The person of color, then, has the perennial challenge of assimilating and achieving Whiteness in order to be worthy, or appropriating what seems White in order to navigate an unjust world to a greater end—that is, eradicating conceptions of inferiority.

Race (via color) only exists because of racism (not the other way around). Frantz Fanon wrote about Black existential psychology in the face of constructions of *inferiority*; we are writing about White existential architectures that constructed and passed on enduring notions of *supremacy*. We model our goal after Fanon's: the point of our analysis is the eradication of supremacy and evolution toward racial justice. Slavery to either inferiority or supremacy is toxic to the ecological health of humanity. The White architecture of the mind, the history of Whiteness, and strategies to maintain dominance are key theoretical components of our argument. They are connected to our proposal of a White evolution of the mind, in pursuit of an ecology of diverse bodies and perspectives.

Higher Learning

As we are university professors, many of our examples throughout the book are set on the college environment. Although we hope that our location in higher education does not preclude these concepts from being applicable in many other situations, we have found that higher education is a contested space where many conversations around diversity and Whiteness occur. Moreover, universities are sites of the knowledge production that has contributed to violence around race and difference.

Conversations about diversity in higher education and in various segments of the workforce are often concerned with predominant Whiteness or predominately White institutions (PWIs). The notion of predominance refers to ratios. Any segment of an organized body that is 51% White is predominately White. In higher education, for example, many institutions are in a rush to achieve 51% non-Whiteness. Institutions are so committed to achieving a non-PWI status that there are new court cases and legislation emerging every year regarding the ability and the degree to which race can be used as a criterion in college admission.[32] Institutions that are far from achieving this 51% status start by claiming victory with a new class of students that is 51% or more non-White. The federal government even offers funding for institutions that have a certain percentage of Latinx students after applying to become a Hispanic Serving Institution (HSIs).

We find the term PWI and the focus on ratios of students to be a weak and misleading unit of analysis. In an effort to consider power structures, historical context, and the influence of other social structures, we refer to dominant Whiteness and Dominantly White Institutions (DWIs), which accounts for the history, location, habits, and proportions of faculty and executives who are White.[33] Focusing on *dominant* as opposed to *predominant* Whiteness creates a framework in which mental architecture and strategies that blot out counter stories and deny privilege become pertinent to understanding diversity.

Higher education is a place where inequality and diversity collide as institutions engage in various methods to expand critical racial consciousness. Educational environments are designed to produce and disseminate knowledge, but schools and colleges are embedded in a society where young people are being lost to state-sanctioned violence. The deaths of Trayvon Martin in 2012 and Michael Brown in 2014 were only two in a series of ongoing tragedies involving the policing of Black men and boys. Earlier in the same year, Eric Garner was killed by a police officer using an illegal choke-hold while Garner repeatedly gasped, "I can't breathe." After Garner and Brown, a young boy, twelve-year-old Tamir Rice, was shot by a police officer who mistook his toy for a weapon. Eric Harris was shot and killed in April 2015 when a reserve officer grabbed his gun instead of a police taser. Two days later, Walter Scott fled from a traffic stop, and video footage shows him being shot from behind. Freddie Gray died of spinal cord injuries only two weeks later because of injuries suffered in a police van. In October 2014, 17-year-old Laquan McDonald was shot sixteen times (nine times in the back) and killed by police in Chicago. In July 2015, Sandra Bland was pulled over for a traffic stop that escalated and led to her arrest; she died in jail three days later. In addition to these police killings of unarmed Black men, women, and children, numerous videos of police forcibly removing Black minors from classrooms, intervening in quarrels, and disbanding neighborhood parties have surfaced, demonstrating an aggressive level of enforcement. The Black Lives Matter movement started after a collection of these events catalyzed a sense of activism throughout the United States.

Most of what we just chronicled involves tragic encounters between Whiteness and Black men and boys. Violence against Black women goes way beyond the death of Sandra Bland, but much of this violence remains invisible, as documented by the *Say Her Name* project out of Columbia Law School.[34] For example, Mya Hall was a Black transgender woman who was killed in 2015 in Baltimore after taking the wrong exit and approaching an NSA building; she was shot and died after crashing into the gate. In contrast to the killings of Eric Garner and Freddie Gray, this incident was written off as involving someone who had a troubled past, which may have served to obscure the fact that police killed an unarmed Black woman.

The Black Lives Matter movement led to the counter-sayings "All Lives Matter" and "White Lives Matter." On university campuses across the country, the Black Lives Matter movement garnered support and catalyzed activism and protest as students felt more compelled to outline their experience at Dominantly White Institutions (DWIs). The activism came to a climax in November 2015 at the University of Missouri, where racial tensions had been growing, a student began a hunger strike, and the football team refused to play until the president resigned. Concurrently, protests took place at Yale University over emails about Halloween costumes, sensitivity, and faculty/staff support, and the student body president and Dean of Students at Claremont McKenna stepped down over similarly embattled issues. More intense variations of this ilk are covered in Chapter 6, entitled White Wrath.

The White responses that exhibit the principles of White out are included throughout the chapters of this book. White student violence, threats of violence, and taunting increased exponentially at the University of Missouri and other places. At a Christian college in the Mid-west, a student drew the Nazi symbol in the snow on cars in a parking lot, and a White president at a DWI wrote a letter to the student body explaining that the university is not a day care or a "safe space," and if students are too sensitive they should attend else-where. Reports of professors using racial slurs in the classroom increased, and claims to academic freedom and the oversensitivity of students were used as a canopy to protect the sacredness of being able to unintentionally demean students of color. The combined weight of these events—and many more—are the context in which White out can be examined as an intentional or unintentional strategy to blot out the counter stories of people of color, who live on the margins or outside of the socially constructed dominant White reality.

There are a variety of ways in which White out can be understood as a byproduct of mental architecture. The often-unconscious purpose in denying privilege and articulating colorblind sameness is intended to support a larger system and view of reality. Moving beyond strategies to reinforce White dominance, we apply an ecological framework to recast an evolution toward racial justice.

Chapter 2, entitled White Pain, is about using claims to pain in a systemic effort to communicate a sameness of experience without regard to race and access to power and privilege. The chapter includes an important distinction between pain that is caused by a system that predisposes certain populations to suffer, as opposed to more randomized acts of violence that likely occur without respect to race. This distinction is a difficult one to make, because pain is personal; however, this is why claims to be in pain become a volatile White-out strategy that obscures the systemic nature of dominant Whiteness.

Chapter 3, Whitefluenza, addresses privilege, an epidemic with no known cure. Here we outline the ever-elusive, incurable, virus-like reality of privilege in a world built on generational wealth, entitlements, and trickle-up economics (the rich are getting richer and the poor are getting poorer). When someone goes to the doctor for advice or treatment about symptoms that feel like the common cold, the diagnosis of a bacterial infection yields the often-sought-after antibiotics, while a viral infection yields the sad realization that the patient is obliged to wait out the symptoms. A virus is a microscopic infectious agent that replicates and mutates inside other living organisms. A virus can spread in many different ways and survive in modular particles when not infecting a host, and antibiotics have no impact. Just as a virus may remain dormant for extended periods of time, only to flare up at critical moments, so Whitefluenza comes to the fore once again to sustain the equilibrium of privilege for those in a dominant position. In the case of some viruses, a healthy immune system can eliminate them, or vaccines can inoculate a host against infection. Similarly, systemic supremacy acts in many of the same ways in promoting and protecting dominant Whiteness—and often operates more effectively when undetected or unacknowledged. The evolution toward supremacy is voracious and tenacious, which means the evolution toward racial justice is going to have to outmatch that tenacity.

Drawing from more of the developmental and individual perspective of Whiteness, Chapter 4, White 22, plays off of Joseph Heller's novel *Catch-22*. It addresses the no-win situations that confront many White individuals daily. There is a great deal of tension between the threat of inactivity in the face of injustice and the liabilities associated with active anti-racist activity that can actually be harmful due to unintended consequences. This chapter explores the evolving role and perception on Whiteness and the desire for right action in the face of a long history of dominance. White 22 is a concept that refers to the "White if you do or White if you don't" tension that exists when White advocates engage in anti-racist activity. The concept addresses the logic system that prevents consciousness raising and the embrace of an interdependent ecosystem.

Chapter 5, entitled Whitroggressions, explores negative attitudes and microaggressions toward Whiteness and even White individuals in order to unpack the role of power and dominance in racist systems and actions. Derogatory racial slurs toward White people and people of color are often perceived differently, but claims of reverse racism function as an attempt to eliminate claims of asymmetry. In this chapter, we highlight emerging depictions of being White in popular culture and in art, including an overview of epithets like "honky" and "cracker." Some White responses to criticism rely on using the same language as people of color, which, combined with stealing pain, serves to White out the reality of asymmetrical experiences. Thus, the concept of Whitroggressions is an important concept that is akin to microaggressions—subtle and cumulative slights against minority identities that are often more acceptable than overt expressions of racism.

In Chapter 6, White Wrath, we turn to the palpable anger that accompanies the evolution from privilege to equality, which can feel like oppression. This anger is highlighted by events like the Oregon standoff with the Bundy brothers, the energy behind the Donald Trump presidential campaigns, the alt-right/White supremacist rally in Charlottesville, and the continued discontent on college campuses, where White student unions have emerged and affirmative action bake sales continue. In order to extract some sense of the dispositional and behavioral shifts resulting from notions of pain claims, Whitefluenza, White 22, and Whitroggressions, Chapter 7, White Noise considers the ways in which White logic creates disruption for evolution toward racial justice, and how White supremacy is manifested even through people of color.

Chapter 8, White Consciousness, offers constructive thoughts about White evolution and shifting dominant White systems through collective critical racial consciousness. The culminating purpose of these concepts is to show that we are an interdependent people. Dominance, supremacy, and oppression in all forms are an assault to our potential for survival as a society comprised of many cultures, epistemologies, knowledges, and histories. True barbarism is a quest for racial purity. Epistemologically and genetically, feeble-mindedness occurs through inbreeding. An ecological evolution toward racial justice and equity is predicated in our recognition of these interlocking principles and a persistent commitment to racial consciousness and fighting against the tendency toward dominance.

Notes

1. "White House Executive Order Prods Colleges on Free Speech, Program-level Data and Risk Sharing." White House Executive Order Prods Colleges on Free Speech, Program-level Data and Risk Sharing. Accessed May 28, 2019. https://www.insidehighered.com/news/2019/03/22/white-house-executive-order-prods-colleges-free-speech-program-level-data-and-risk.

2. For a lengthy and full treatment of this history and ideas, see Painter, Nell Irvin. *The History of White People*. New York: W. W. Norton, 2011.

3. Notes on the State of Virginia by Thomas Jefferson, edited by William Peden. University of North Carolina Press, 1982, p. 143.

4. For an extensive discussion of Eugenics, see: "Race and Membership in American History: The Eugenics Movement." *Facing History, Facing Ourselves*, 2002. Accessed April 18, 2019. https://www.facinghistory.org/sites/default/files/publications/Race_Membership.pdf.

5. Ibid.

6. https://www.flickr.com/photos/ntugetaiwan/41496704081/in/photolist-22wwqkB-6Ak-LNy-6AgECr-6AkLn9-6AkMym-6AgFHZ-6AkL85-6AgFQD-6AgDuv-dG9tES-6Ak-L4h-6AgDct-8J3tRw-oeZ5k5-6AkLyh-6AkL1h-XiMTXh-6AkLiy-28zwaDB-HiipiX-5TkeMb-bHdU8R-fJ17Mt-nYHUQd-29NhmCj-nDM4nC-eVxJ4n-28tL9Bm-9DBnJM-6bf9EZ-fJ81Ku-5VhYfd-q4zNbw-cMs1Ej-26dVspc-dW5km4-6dXeur-oeZq1L-7u4mpN-nsiaZF-8yV8AM-5cjRb9-fJfYEQ-qnPZsp-dC7MQG-J1N3vL-5VdAae-ouvM8N-8j3PVx-9fWg24.

7. Minium, Alice. "The Untold Story of American Eugenics." *Medium*. April 15, 2018. Accessed April 18, 2019. https://medium.com/@aliceminium/the-feebleminded-woman-a-brief-history-of-eugenics-in-1920s-america-8a198d1b6e40.

8. "Fannie Lou Hamer." *PBS*. Accessed May 28, 2019. https://www.pbs.org/wgbh/americanexperience/features/freedomsummer-hamer/.

9. See more on this reporting in: Wells, Ida (1892). "Southern Horrors: Lynch Law in All Its Phases—Preface". *Digital History*. University of Houston. Retrieved March 10, 2019 from http://www.digitalhistory.uh.edu/disp_textbook.cfm?smtid=3&psid=3614.

10. Arthur B. Stout (1862) https://archive.org/details/chineseimmigrati0000stou/page/22.

11. Zelikovsky, Joy. "Intergenerational Transmission of Trauma among Holocaust Survivors." *PsycEXTRA Dataset*, 2014. doi:10.1037/e556222014-001.

12. Jansen, Jonathan D. *Knowledge in the Blood: Confronting Race and the Apartheid Past*. Cape Town: UCT Press, 2013.

13. "Race and Membership in American History: The Eugenics Movement." *Facing History, Facing Ourselves*, 2002. Accessed April 18, 2019. https://www.facinghistory.org/sites/default/files/publications/Race_Membership.pdf.

14. Black, Edwin. "Eugenics and the Nazis—the California Connection." *SFGate*. January 15, 2012. Accessed March 27, 2019. https://www.sfgate.com/opinion/article/Eugenics-and-the-Nazis-the-California-2549771.php.

15. Fanon, Frantz; Translated from the French by Richard Philcox. *Black Skin, White Masks*. New York: Grove Press, 2008. p. xvi.

16. Freire, Paulo, and Donaldo Macedo. *Pedagogy of the Oppressed*. New York: Bloomsbury Academic, 2018. p. 108.

17. Colored is a distinct racial category in South Africa that came to mean "mixed race." A placard on chameleons, those who changed their racial classification, is featured in the Apartheid Museum in Johannesburg, South Africa linking back to a news article in the *Johannesburg Star* on March 21, 1986.

18. Santos, Boaventura De Sousa. *The End of the Cognitive Empire: The Coming of Age of Epistemologies of the South*. Durham: Duke University Press, 2018.

19. Berger, Peter L., Thomas Luckmann, and Dariuš Zifonun. *The Social Construction of Reality*. New York: Random House, na, 2002. *The Social Construction of Reality* is particularly informative, as is it conveys a framework in which dominant views of reality attempt to assimilate or annihilate competing views of reality. A perspective becomes dominant through a process of habituation and legitimation and is then conferred as reality. The notion that it is socially constructed points to the fact that it can be created and destroyed and so does not have an objective and value-neutral status. It is still a reality because it influences how people think and behave, and it positions them in relationship to the structure that supports that reality.

20. Roediger, David R. *Working toward Whiteness: How America's Immigrants Became White: The Strange Journey from Ellis Island to the Suburbs*. New York: Basic Books, 2006. Roediger's book outlines the legal process for Dagos and Wasps becoming White and the economic effects this had on other immigrant groups with darker skin tones.

21. Thomas, Roosevelt R., and Marjorie I. Woodruff. *Building a House for Diversity*. New York: AMACOM, 1999. The book begins with this fable that sets the stage for an application to diversity in various contexts.

22. Kahneman, Daniel. *Thinking, Fast and Slow*. London: Macmillan, 2011. Kahneman's work is a thorough and empirical look at two general ways of thinking.

23. Müller-Lyer, Franz Carl. Optische Urteilstäuschungen. DuboisReymonds Archiv für Anatomie und Physiologie, Supplement Volume, 1889. 263–270.

24. "Project Implicit". Accessed September 20, 2015, https://implicit.harvard.edu/ implicit/ education.html.

25. Clark, Kenneth Bancroft and Mamie Phipps Clark. "Racial Identification and Preference in Negro Children." *Readings in Social Psychology* 19, no. 3 (1950): 341–350.

26. "White and Black Children Biased toward Lighter Skin," *CNN.com*, last modified May 14, 2010, http://www.cnn.com/2010/US/05/13/doll.study/.

27. Fanon, p. 138.

28. Fanon, p. 127.

29. hooks, bell. *Talking Back: Thinking Feminist, Thinking Black.* Boston, MA: South End Press, 1989, 113.

30. Hill-Collins, Patricia, and Sirma Bilge. *Intersectionality.* Chicester: John Wiley & Sons, 2016, 2. We draw from the following definition of intersectionality: "When it comes to social inequality, people's lives and the organizations of power in a given society are better understood as being shaped not by a single axis of social division, be it race or gender or class, but by many axes that work together and influence each other. Intersectionality as an analytic tool gives people better access to the complexity of the world and of themselves."

31. Du Bois, William Edward Burghardt, and Brent Hayes Edwards. *The Souls of Black Folk.* Oxford: Oxford University Press, 2008.

32. *Fisher v. The University of Texas (Fisher II)* is the latest, but was preceded by *Gratz v. Bollinger* and *Grutter v. Bollinger* at the University of Michigan. The general rule is that it can be loosely applied but not as a major criterion.

33. Gusa, Diane Lynn. "White Institutional Presence: The Impact of Whiteness on Campus Climate." *Harvard Educational Review* 80, no. 4 (2010): 464–490. See Gusa's discussion of White Institutional Presence (WIP) for more about the culture of a campus and the way it includes or excludes various epistemologies and ideologies.

34. Crenshaw, Kimberlé, Andrea J. Ritchie, Rachel Anspach, Rachel Gilmer, and Luke Harris. *Say Her Name: Resisting Police Brutality against Black Women.* New York: The African American Policy Forum, 2015.

· 2 ·

WHITE PAIN: "I HURT, TOO"

Over the years, while traveling to and speaking at college campuses across the country to engage in conversations on racial injustice, we have noticed a phenomenon that often occurs whenever White people engage in discussions about racism and Whiteness. When people of color begin to share their painful lived experiences and examples of systemic racism, some White folks respond to stories of racialized pain with their own stories of hurt, pain, suffering, and loss. We acknowledge that systems of racism tie together the pain of the oppressor and oppressed;[1] however, White pain combined with other systems of dominance based and discriminatory barriers like gender, class, ability, or status can serve to delegitimize the racialized pain that many people of color endure within the systems of racialized oppression.

White pain, then, is a pattern of how White folks, either unwittingly or with passive-aggressive defensive intentionality, claim their own pain in the foreground of a discussion on race, to the exclusion and erasure of pain that racialized others face. I (Jun) recall a particularly heated exchange when a White male colleague, upon hearing several other colleagues share emotional stories of racism and misogyny, voiced his concern to the group. He blurted aloud, as his faced slowly turned crimson, "I hurt, too!" He went on to share how he was robbed and the assailants were never charged, tried, or convicted.

His personal pain was very real, very devastating, and worthy of empathy and compassion. Yet I could not help but wonder if the "I hurt, too" trope also functions in discussions like this as a way of diffusing White responsibility in the face of systemic racialized pain. In other words, not all pain is the same.

In conversations about racial injustice, pain claims are never neutral. What does it mean to steal down another's pain? How do we deal with the realities of White pain when navigating conversations about race and racism? What are the motivations behind the need to share a story of deep personal pain in response to stories shared by others about systemic racism? Moreover, what is the impact of White pain responses that ultimately serve to defend White dominance in the face of racialized pain for people of color? The observable pattern demonstrates that White logic programs an individual's response to recollections of systemic racism with stories of individual pain such as family alcoholism, divorce, weight gain, or childhood bullying. Although we seek to understand the intent behind such remarks, we know that the impact is ultimately an erasure and negation of the pain that people of color systematically face, and an extended defense of White dominance.

This is a difficult concept to convey. Some forms of pain are connected to identities that are coupled with systemic oppression and violence (e.g. poverty, sexual abuse, and others). Distinguishing between personal White pain as a defense of White dominance and acknowledging systemic oppression where it operates is a complex and unclear process. This tension occurs in other areas as well, such as with intersecting identities (see Chapter 3 on Whitefluenza). The complexity is most perilous when an attempt is made to point out White pain (which potentially recreates the oppression of other identities).

A central tenet of Critical Race Theory (CRT) is the need to distinguish between intent versus impact.[2] The intersecting nature of intent and impact is a fundamental justice issue. If a grocery store patron runs over the feet of a fellow shopper with a cart and offers as an explanation, "I did not mean to hurt you," this does not change the damage that was done, and it does not remove the consequences that may result. Similarly, if the unwitting offender immediately begins telling a story about when they too were once run over by an errant cart, or otherwise hurt in some way, this does not change the impact of that event for the injured. Even worse, the script may be flipped and the blame is shifted to the victim when the offender offers an explanation about the consequences of standing in the middle of the supermarket aisle. This, too, would exacerbate the pain. "I apologize if you were hurt while standing in my way" is no apology, no excuse, and no way to make amends after an avoidable offense. When people say or do something that is racist, sexist, or homophobic, they often defend their own motivations first, thereby attempting to divorce their impact from their intent. But the intent of one person does not matter as much as the impact on the other.

The White pain claim, in response to hearing stories of racialized pain and injustice, should be evaluated through the lens of *impact* more than *intent*. Initially, our simplistic assessment of these perplexing responses was that expressing White pain was rooted in assessing the psychological need to shift the conversation away from the burden of White guilt. In truth, there are an infinite number of motivations for these types of responses, and indeed what might be at work is far more complex. Perhaps it could be a disappointment that the mythical promise of White supremacy has not been fulfilled. In addition to turning away from guilt, White pain (even when legitimate), might also be deployed as a strategy to diffuse responsibility for being complicit in systems of inter-structured oppression. Our point is that White pain, when used in this way, can serve to erase the systems of pain at work in the lives of people of color, and that Whites systematically benefit from this erasure, irrespective of intent. Although it is true that sharing painful stories can be an attempt to join in solidarity with the pain of racialized *others*, it is also true that the impact of "I hurt, too" responses is rooted in denying others' pain. Consequently, through implying that they have had it worse, White people ultimately convey to people of color that they should stop complaining.

White logic systems perpetuate dominance through attempts to delegitimize expressions of oppression. A key feature of oppressive systems is the ability to either force a competing definition of reality to assimilate or to annihilate it. By gaslighting and insinuating, "you are making it up," the White dominant reality forces the oppressed person experiencing pain to second guess their reality and either assimilate or face further alienation. Offering examples of White pain is an attempt at equalizing and therefore invalidating. White pain as an individual expression, signals and communicates the position of power in a White logic system.

Empathy and Solidarity

The work of diversity, equity, and inclusion often emphasizes the role of empathy and solidarity. A generous interpretation of White pain as a response to racialized oppression may appear as an attempt at genuine caring and support for a hurting friend. In other words, the "I hurt, too" response can be an attempt at solidarity. For example, when Asian colleagues share a difficult racialized experience, White colleagues might want to be empathetic to their colleague. The "I hurt, too" response can be about joining with the humanity of another. If White colleagues cannot fully understand where a Black colleagues' pain comes from, they might dig inward and find their own pain in order to serve as a bridge to their colleagues. If other forms of progress follow the initial feeling of empathy, then this concept of stealing down pain is an initial step on a developmental journey.

Over time, we have heard many White students, colleagues, and workshop attendees respond to racialized pain with stories of childhood trauma and other stories of suffering. In response to the stories of racism that their colleagues of color share, they respond with their own stories of pain. That first time we heard a student share a painful (yet unrelated to diversity) story, we were shocked; the collective focus of our conversation so quickly shifted toward addressing and empathizing with the individual and her pain that it simultaneously de-emphasized the focus of racialized pain that was initially shared. However, it turned out that *each time* we engaged in deep and meaningful dialogue around racism, someone invariably would steal down the pain of others, and share her or his own painful stories—of something, anything, other than racial injustice. Perhaps the vulnerable moments experienced as a group in a safe space elicit a deeper unconscious feeling of a need to share something painful for the good of the order. However, when someone shares a story of divorce in the context of a diversity and social justice class, the driving logic and rationale is unclear. In fact, each time a story of deep grief and anguish was shared, the conversation shifted to appropriately address that individual's emotional need and state of vulnerability. There seemed to be a collective desire to cut these people some slack. They hurt, too. They clearly have experienced deep pain.

After several years, it was clear to us that this trend was pervasive—White people sharing and claiming their individual pains in response to examples of systemic pain among people of color. Again, regardless of the intent of those who share their pain stories, the net effect is that these stories detract from the pain of lived experiences for people of color. When we witness people digging into their emotional storage and pulling out the experience of divorce in response to someone talking about a racial microaggression, we realize that there is a larger underlying phenomenon. In the setting of a class or a workshop, revealing an experience of family violence may seem appropriate, but it is also an indication of downplaying or ignoring systemic racism that happens to millions of people of color over the last two hundred years. The reactive response is often unconscious, but it is clearly White out—an attempt (even if unintended) to blot out one person's experience with a different heavy and emotional experience. "My pain is worse than your pain." It is stealing down the pain. "Your pain, I acknowledge, but mine is greater; therefore, you have no reason to be upset": this logic may be the underbelly of meritocracy. Although the empathy may be genuine, it may also be a proxy for conveying, "Oh, you hurt? So do I. Oh, someone called you n[word]? I got robbed." So, whose pain is worse? Who gets more sympathy in the classroom or another social space? In the end, stealing down the pain serves to invalidate another's legitimate pain claim related to race.

White-upping the Other

Swapping war stories, playing a perpetual game of one-upping (or White-upping, as it were), may be part of the White logic system that drives these types of responses to people of color. Prisoners might do this about their escapades that led them to prison. New parents might engage in this behavior among friends, talking about child rearing, their children's messy bowel movements, sleep deprivation, and whatever crazy thing happened on the airplane. We have seen young men one-up each other as part of daily locker room banter. So, one component of White-upping and stealing down the pain is a natural inclination to tell a better story in order to be competitive. White-upping is a defense mechanism whereby White people, uncomfortable with stories of racism from people of color, steal pain by disclosing their own individual pain. This behavior can be an unconscious and unintentional response; still, it is important to recognize the distinctions between an individual's pain, where a stratified society did not condition or predispose the experience, and the pain derived from a systemic injustice. Stealing pain serves to defend White dominance by rejecting systemic pain claims.

I (Jun) recall a conversation I had with some graduate students several years ago. One student was sharing about her experiences of being the only Black woman in school, and being called a variety of racially derogatory slurs. She proceeded to share her story from the fifth grade about being called n[word] and people touching her hair. A White male colleague jumped in and shared that when he played basketball in high school, he was the *only* White player, and everybody called him White Shadow. His ultimate claim was, "So, I understand where you are coming from." He failed to recognize the systemic and perpetual nature of racism she experienced. In refusing to acknowledge her pain, he stole her pain; by disputing pain claims, he obscured the systemic nature of the experiences. This conversation serves as an example of the "I also can relate to your pain because this happened to me too" competition. Although externally claiming, "I hurt, too," the intent behind his comment was not one of empathy. He did not try to relate to her. He was merely communicating that she was not the only one who has suffered.

Defensive pain claims can occur anonymously, or at least at a distance, through social media. A primary example of these claims occurred at the University of Missouri in 2015 and at other sites of protest where tolerance for racial inequity is waning. As a response to ongoing racism on campus, some students went on hunger strikes and held demonstrations and rallies across the campus calling for the resignation of the university's president. The football team then decided to boycott (first the Black players and then eventually the entire team). The boycott preceded the eventual resignation of both the university's president as well as the University of Missouri system's chancellor. The critiques of this movement and countless others like it on social media have conveyed a consistent theme: students today are too sensitive, too politically correct, and are being coddled.

Figure 2.1 is similar to a meme found on Alaska governor Sarah Palin's Facebook page, which included her comment, "YOUR BRAIN ON COLLEGE: WUSSIFIED WHINERS PROVE WHAT A WASTE IT'S

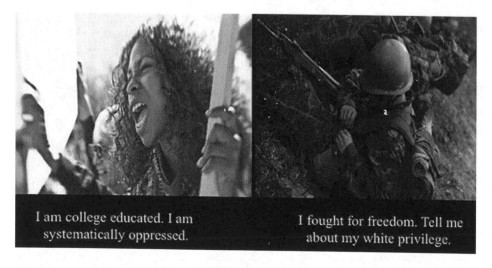

I am college educated. I am systematically oppressed.

I fought for freedom. Tell me about my white privilege.

Figure 2.1: A Replica of "Wussified Whiners" by Sarah Palin

BECOMING." This image and the embedded comments encapsulated the essence of pain claims through an "I hurt, too" message meant to shut down the claims of others. The convenient comparison in this case is between a college student who started a hunger strike to create awareness of racial injustices, and a WWII soldier who died for his country. It is ironic that the American military at the time of the second Great War to end fascism in Europe had segregated units, which simply mirrored the ongoing pre-civil rights Jim Crow laws back home in the United States. The "I hurt, too" mentality here encapsulates White feelings of frustration with and trivialization of the complaints of people of color.

Emotional Appropriation

Rachel Dolezal,[3] the former president of the National Association for the Advancement of Colored People (NAACP) chapter in Spokane, Washington, made news in the summer of 2015 with the revelation (by her White parents) that she is not Black. She grew up with four adopted Black siblings and developed a great sense of passion for the Black experience. Eventually, she went to Howard University, married a Black man, and at some point, began adjusting her physical appearance (hair style and skin tone) to look Black. One response to her identity presentation was that it was a deeper level of Blackface and cultural appropriation. During the same summer, Caitlyn Jenner had just presented herself to the world as a woman. A variety of voices criticized those who supported Jenner and not Dolezal, asking why is it acceptable to change your gender and/or sex and not your racial identity? As it pertains to the notion of stealing pain, a key event in Dolezal's life was her legal suit against Howard University for damages based on alleged discrimination, including her race—White.[4] The transition from identifying as White and the allegations for discrimination based on being White is one fraught with questions about the motivation and intent. This case is pertinent to concepts in Chapter 3, but it exemplifies a complicated notion of appropriating or even stealing pain followed by a guise of sameness.

Injustice versus Systemic Injustice

There are multiple interpretations of the word injustice. Consider when someone says, "The perpetrator never came to justice, so I know what you mean when you say you were oppressed." One problem with a statement like this is that it becomes a game of *oppression Olympics*. Who really deserves the gold medal of sympathy? Who's really had the most challenging course? We acknowledge that an individual caused great pain. It is horrible and tragic, and may even be considered an injustice. Recounting those memories will evoke empathy in most listeners. However, it was not *systemic* in the same way acts of racism, sexism, and homophobia are perpetuated at both the individual and structural level.

Although the possession of a White architecture of the mind is an individualized application, the concept is systemic in that the architectural design is a product of a dominant system. The point is that the architecture of the mind is linked to a larger system of influence. The internalization of blueprints represents the interactions between individuals and the perpetuation of the system, which always finds new ways to deal with attempts to invalidate it. Saying "I hurt, too" erases the significance of systemic injustices and the systems that perpetuate them. One White person's isolated, yet painful, experience does not measure the same as the Black, Latinx, Indigenous, or Asian experience, which represents generations of enslavement, oppression, laws created to prevent economic, physical, and psychological well-being in the form of Jim Crow laws, redlining in the real estate market, immigration restrictions, eugenics, exclusion acts, and the resultant subpar public education. An isolated violation of one person's individual right to safety is not the same as the generational consequences of genocide and land theft on Indigenous Americans, the illegal occupation of the sovereign Hawai'i, or of Japanese American internment following WWII. In the White architecture of the mind, individualistic evaluations are pervasive, and they tend to avoid or White out systemic issues where an individual is predisposed toward a certain outcome based on their social location.

As an extension of the difference between individual and systemic racism, there is a distinction between prejudice and racism. Prejudice consists of individual assumptions and preconceived notions that are often negative and applied toward certain groups, including implicit and explicit biases. Prejudice is different from racism in that racism is individual prejudice multiplied by power.[5] Racism is therefore systemic prejudice that involves power as a key dynamic in dominance.

Black Lives Matter? All Lives Matter!

Following an immense amount of media coverage, the subject of Black Lives Matter vs. All Lives Matter made its way into a question in the first democratic presidential primary debate in 2015. The expression "All Lives Matter" had by that time emerged as a retort to the Black Lives Matter movement. Claiming that *all* lives matter ostensibly asserts that there is some level of equity in our country, or that everybody has the same opportunity. However, an examination of whether or not "all lives (really) matter" is quickly resolved with an examination of prison rates, incarceration rates, income inequality, and educational access across the population. Presidential candidate Bernie Sanders responded to the question about Black Lives Matter in this way:

> Anderson Cooper: From Arthur in Des Moines: Do black lives matter or do all lives matter? Let's put that question to Senator Sanders.
> Bernie Sanders: Black lives matter, and the reason those words matter is the African American community knows that on any given day, some innocent person like Sandra Bland can get into a car, and then three days later she's going to end up dead in jail or their kids are gonna get shot. We need to combat institutional racism from top to bottom, and we need major, major reforms in a broken criminal justice system in which we have more people in jail than China. I intend to tackle that issue to make sure that our people have education and jobs rather than jail cells.[6]

Daryl Smith[7] and other scholars on diversity have likewise expressed the importance of remaining focused on the unfinished work of centuries-long struggles against systemic oppression in the U.S.

Our focus on Whiteness does not serve as a disavowal that there are other discriminatory barriers to social justice. We are drawn to race because it embodies an intersectional complexity and we want to orient our discussion of justice around race because of the centuries of unfinished work in this arena. In the context of pain claims about issues other than race (like weight, ability, or gender), we acknowledge the work of Smith, Crenshaw, and others in situating race as one piece of a composite effort toward supremacy and injustice.[8] The role of gender, for example, is fundamentally important and intricately interwoven into conceptualizing race. However, when White women default to *only* gender, or even gender first, within their pain claims, it subordinates the role of race within that intersectionality and the systemic and perpetual

injustices of racism. It is a subtle yet destructive approach to derailing discussions of race, because it denies and waters down the role of race and its
influence in society. Other categories of social inequality combine uniquely
with the role of Whiteness to manifest some form of dominance: for example,
being White and gay, White and female, or White and poor still ultimately
centers Whiteness.

White supremacy is insidious and harmful in both secular and sacred
spaces. Whiteness and White culture include White people, but it is also a
system that is designed to allow White logic to intentionally or unintentionally hurt others as a result of being authentic or having a voice in the diversity
conversation. Systems produce logic and individuals contribute to systems.
The mutual benefits of Whiteness to individuals and systems are built into the
DNA of supremacy. White folks can be particularly sensitive when it comes
to discussions of racial inequity. In the opening chapter of this book we shared
the parable of the elephant and giraffe, where the elephant was left pondering
if a house intended for giraffes would ever be welcoming for elephants. In the
next section, we extend the metaphor to incorporate more complexities of
White pain.

White People: Porcupines of the Wilderness

Have you ever seen a porcupine? They have dart-like quills, and if you tried to
embrace the animal, there would be painful repercussions. Since their quills
are a defense mechanism, the release of their built-in weaponry may be both
voluntary or involuntary. Their sharp quills become elevated and poised for
attack when they are feeling threatened. This intimidating stance becomes
their natural defensive posture. Similarly, the idea that when White people
respond to discussions on race with anger or defensiveness, believing it is
simply part of "who they are" may bring some measure of understanding to
colleagues of color, and maybe even a level of justification for White people.
When they feel threatened, White people will get defensive; and that is when
they can become truly dangerous (see more on White aggression and wrath
in Chapter 6). White defensiveness can also lie dormant for extended periods
of time (see more on this in Chapter 3, on White supremacy as a virus) and
re-emerge unexpectedly.

"Not all porcupines!" some may naturally retort. Some porcupines might
believe that they have been wrongly villainized and targeted and are therefore
a potential endangered species. Porcupines are the real victims! This defense

of White dominance occurs through contradictory communication and is, in some ways, also predictable. The White architecture of the mind and its logical byproducts yield a set of conditions whereby White people can produce the feelings of victimization in discussions of racial equity while simultaneously criticizing a victim mentality in others. When you are accustomed to privilege, equity feels like oppression.

While some porcupines will concur, others are going to believe that if they are nice enough, and if they mean well, and if they never intentionally try to hurt other animals, then they should neither be vilified nor feared. A major problem with this line of thinking goes back to the systemic rather than individualistic. A porcupine will at some point always revert to being a porcupine. Should we eliminate all porcupines from the earth, as some may suggest? Will that solve the problem, or shall we begin a dismantling campaign to de-quill all the porcupines? Of course not. The nihilistic, no-win mentality leads to the question, is there no hope for White participation? A key to healthy participation for porcupines comes in recognizing their own potential danger to the work of equity. And committed White participation means recognizing their position and privilege, recognizing when helping can hurt, and a deep commitment to an evolving racial consciousness.

As with all analogies, the illustration of the porcupine inevitably breaks down; but the example of the porcupine offers a helpful addition to the previous parable of the elephant and giraffe. In that story, the giraffe designs an architecture that is built around his own kind and then blames the elephant for not fitting in. Of course, the psychological term for this is gaslighting. Blaming the oppressed and then claiming they are leveraging a debilitating victim mentality is akin to emotional abuse.

Emotional abuse is usually something that takes place between two individuals; but it can also serve as a metaphor for analyzing systemic language. Gaslighting is a form of emotional abuse in which abusers deny the experiences and perceptual reality of their victims, making the latter think they are the irrational ones. After experiencing gaslighting, someone may seriously question their own understanding. Gaslighting favors the abuser—or, in the case of systemic justice, the oppressor. The goal of gaslighting is to make someone feel that their perceptions of reality are wrong. It can come in the form of a calm voice, disposition, and persona, requesting that someone who has experienced trauma or pain to respond in a calm, civil, and inclusive manner. Telling someone who is hurt to stop overreacting is a form of abuse—or, in its systemic form, oppression.

White folks engaged in racial justice work might erroneously imagine they can "shed" their Whiteness, or they might embrace the message that they are somehow "down for the cause," or that their colleagues of color will stop seeing them as White. But to think this way defeats the whole purpose of evolving toward a state of critical consciousness. The reality is that for people of color engaged in justice work, White people will always pose a certain amount of danger. Some quill-punctures are intentional while others are not; but in the end, people of color will inevitably get hurt by White people. It is the way the architecture of White supremacy manifests in reality. Learning that defense mechanisms can be weaponized is one way a porcupine can adapt to reducing the damage by living in fear. Learning and unlearning thought patterns and behaviors is part of striving toward consciousness.

Smirk or Smile? Epitome of White Pain

When you observe a racially charged incident, what do you see, what do you assume, and how does that guide your sense of who is culpable? Covington Catholic High School is a dominantly White, private high school in Kentucky. One student, Nick Sandmann, found himself at the center of the storm of politics that divide the U.S. A media frenzy surrounded this high schooler, who was caught on video sporting a red hat that said "Make America Great Again" and standing face to face with a Native American man tapping a drum. In the summary of the stories, it appeared that Nick, along with many other high school boys in MAGA hats, were antagonizing the man. The students were on a trip with their high school to attend a rally to oppose abortion. At the end of the day, a collision of interests and identities was captured on film and presented in piecemeal ways through media outlets. School officials, religious leaders, and media outlets condemned the boys and Nick Sandmann for being disrespectful, based on the footage of the boys jumping around and doing school chants, and of Nick standing provocatively with a peculiar look on his face while an indigenous man was calmly chanting and tapping a drum.

But this was not the whole story. What the media summaries and the initial reactions missed was the fact that while the boys were waiting for transportation at the end of the day, a group of Black Hebrew Israelites were engaged in a small demonstration nearby. The presence of the White Catholic school boys in MAGA hats drew commentary from the demonstrators about the boys, their hats, and their support of President Trump. One of the demonstrators even said a boy in the student group had the face of a school shooter.

The words of the Black Hebrew Israelites, in turn, provoked the boys to jump around, chant, and take on the taunts. One of the boys even took his shirt off and rallied his classmates in a school chant, to the cheering encouragement of his classmates. After this went on for a few minutes, a tribal elder named Nathan Phillips slow-walked in between the Black Hebrew Israelites and the boys while chanting his own song. Some of the boys filmed, some moved, and one boy stood his ground, with a frozen expression and the corners of his lips slightly turned upwards, eyes locked on the drumming man in close proximity. It appeared to be a stare-down of sorts, and it went viral. What followed online was first condemnation of the boys—and then a backlash against the reactionary condemners for not telling the whole story.

The Racial Rorschach Test

The crux of the story often re-centers Sandmann's face, his expressions, and the question of what he was doing—was he smirking, or was he smiling? What is the difference between the two expressions? The late ethnographer Clifford Geertz once posed the question, what is the difference between a blink and wink? The differences are context, intent, and impact. As many commentators such as Matt Beauchamp state, one's interpretation of the incident is akin to a racial Rorschach test, revealing what political predispositions and perspectives color your own lens.[9] Imagine the development of a racial Rorschach test designed to reveal logical arguments, systems, and internal coding. Until the logic system is decoded, it cannot be reconstructed. In the notion of racial Rorschach test, the face of Nick Sandmann has generated a plethora of polarizing responses. Was he smiling (innocently) or smirking (with malice)?

Any viral story has a subsequent set of viral reactions. Posts of memes with Nick's face included the words "I see it as a smile," while others included "Smirking White Boy," as shown if Figure 2.2.[10] Still others compared the event to another national news story about the confirmation fight for Supreme Court nominee Brett Kavanaugh, who was accused of sexual assault by Dr. Christine Blasey Ford. The accusation dated back to their high school years. Opinions about the appropriateness of a dated accusation, the evidence, the pain of victims, the pain of accusations, and the timing of the revelation during the Supreme Court nomination hearings were all the subject of fierce debate.

On one hand, in the cases of Sandmann and Kavanaugh we witnessed a high school boy and a man accused of doing something while in high school,

Figure 2.2: Smirking Whiteboy by Robert What (used with permission of artist)

both at the center of a national debate. The parallel is even more apparent in that these two White males, both associated with Donald Trump, eventually took on the disposition of a victim, at least in the eyes of their supporters. Sandmann was portrayed and defended as a dutiful citizen who was vilified by social justice warriors, while Kavanaugh was portrayed as an honorable public servant who was attacked by the left liberal media and feminists. There was also much discussion online and elsewhere regarding the "looks" on their faces—was that a knowing smirk, or a genuine smile?

On the other hand, the conservative political affiliations of these two men left some onlookers feeling licensed to attack them. Trump supporters have been documented shouting "Make America great again!" and wearing Trump paraphernalia while at the same time chanting, "Build that wall!" and other inflammatory ideas related to immigration, race, ability, and religion. As a result, these slogans and paraphernalia are taken to be presumptively offensive. The cultivated conservative image (and its corresponding ideology) became the "mistreated" because of their support of Trump. For example, a conservative play on words for "hate crimes" has become "hat crimes," in reference to those judged for wearing MAGA hats. Similarly, references to the threat of hypocritical progressives who oppose Trump and who police ideologies have been linked to a quote in George Orwell's dystopian book, *1984*:

It was terribly dangerous to let your thoughts wander when you were in any public place or within range of a telescreen. The smallest thing could give you away. A nervous tic, an unconscious look of anxiety, a habit of muttering to yourself—anything that carried with it the suggestion of abnormality, of having something to hide. In any case, to wear an improper expression on your face (to look incredulous when a victory was announced, for example) was itself a punishable offense. There was even a word for it in Newspeak: facecrime, it was called. (p.55)

Instead of hate crimes then, the real threat becomes *hat crimes*, or *face crimes*.

In reference to Nick, the logic of one argument runs toward sympathy for his pain. "This poor kid," it goes; "he went to the nation's capital in his red 'Make America Great Again' cap, seeking to defend the rights of the unborn—yet he became vilified as a racist and White supremacist with a 'punchable face.' All he did was smile and 'stand his ground.'"

The White logic system of those who were quick to defend the actions of this adolescent and his friends reminds us of others who could not wait to engage in White pain, to declare that they hurt too. In fact, the Sandmann family hurt so much over this that they sued CNN and *The Washington Post* for libel and slander. In one case they settled out of court for what was reported to be a very large sum of money. This highlights the ultimate victim mentality—that the one truly hurt by our system was a White kid wearing a MAGA hat. But the actions of the students are supported only by a selective analysis and rhetoric: He was just a boy standing still (not a White privileged boy, from a White privileged Catholic school, standing in a mob of White men being sent to protest medical interventions/procedures/decisions that largely impact the bodies of women, wearing a MAGA hat, staring down a Native American elder). If he had been a Black boy staring that way at a White police officer, there is evidence to suggest he could have been beaten, if not shot.

In the spirit of twisting phrases, we intend for our work on consciousness to Make America Think Again. The irony is that in this case the "victimized" White boy was standing his ground—and "stand your ground" was the same phrase used to legally justify the shooting of an unarmed Black boy by a neighborhood watch coordinator who apparently felt threatened by a bag of Skittles and a hoodie.[11] Claims of political and ideological oppression are coming from the party in power under a president, who has made disparaging comments along a variety of lines and offered conciliatory remarks about White nationalist protesters in Charlottesville (more on this in Chapter 6, White wrath).

The same scrutiny is not applied by police officers who feel threatened by the *appearance* of Black boys. *Threat perception* can lead to violence and death and justify the use of force. Consider Tamir Rice, the twelve-year-old

Black boy sitting in a park, unarmed, who was shot and killed—murdered by a police officer who faced no real consequences for his actions. Steve Loomis, an experienced officer and representative of the police union, was speaking about the case of Tamir Rice and said, "Any officer would have done the same thing"—much to the shock and offense of the journalist, Sarah Koenig, who was interviewing him. She resisted his sentiment and said:

> **Koenig:** You wouldn't have done the same thing. You're telling me right now you wouldn't have.
> **Loomis:** In Tamir Rice, I absolutely would have done the same thing.
> **Koenig:** You would not have done the same thing.
> **Loomis:** I absolutely would have done the same thing.[12]

The journalist reflected on the firm stance of killing a twelve-year-old because of his appearance, size, and weight and added that this is why so many people in Cleveland believe the police there have no willingness to self-reflect or self-correct. But this is the same society that is cultivating the mentality that Sandmann is a victim because of *the way he looks* and that the police are justified in eliminating perceived threats—because of *the way they look*.

As a final note on this point about perception and culpability, the Georgetown Law Center on Poverty and Inequality produced a groundbreaking report on the erasure of childhood for Black girls.[13] The primary finding of the large study was that adults view Black girls as less innocent and more adult-like than their White peers. The implication of this profoundly disparaging perception is that Black girls are perceived to need less nurturing, protection, support, and comfort, and that they know more about adult topics like sex and are independent. The theory of adultification and the accompanying culpability assigned to children who are perceived as adults show a massive disadvantage toward Black girls, and lead to social and educational institutions becoming punitive environments where these girls are 20% more likely to be disciplined and punished than their White peers. The study shows that race is a key factor in determining culpability and perceptions of adulthood—meaning, the way they look.

Evolving and Cultivating Consciousness

The way people look translates to real-life advantages and disadvantages in a racial caste system. The racial Rorschach test is essential in the development of racial consciousness—what do you see, what do you assume, and how does that guide your sense of who is culpable? Furthermore, the test exposes where pain is perceived, manufactured, and manipulated. The same White pain casts Sandmann as a victim and Tamir Rice as someone who is a threat.

We argue in this chapter that White folks can become conscious of the ways they erase the pain of others through stories of their own White pain. What matters here is not choosing acceptable language and word-policing, but rather an awareness of systems and our participation in them. The notion of *colonizing* pain, while discussed here as an individual act, can be interrogated in greater depth from a systemic perspective. White people have been imprinted with a way of encountering race problems in the United States from a dominant position for so long that, even without intending to do so, they extract emotional resources from those with less power.

White folks can learn the art of *holding another's pain.* When people of color are racialized and suffer the consequences of White supremacy, friends from the dominant group should just listen and embrace the pain, rather than rationalize, justify, dismiss, or explain alternative reasons for their pain. Moreover, people in a dominant group need to develop strategies of holding another's pain in the same way that they hold their own pain. This is especially true as they occupy dominant space in conversations about racial injustice. White folks in dominant spaces should absolutely recognize, share, and hold onto their own pain; yet they ought to also ensure that even as they hold on to their own pain, they simultaneously place the systemic pain of racialized "others" in the forefront of the discussion. Failure to do so may unwittingly contribute to defending White dominance, and will ultimately continue to erase the racialized pain that people of color experience, not only as individuals but also as part of an enduring systemic reality for multiple generations.

So, for example, whenever a student or colleague's contribution to a discussion on racial injustice centers a personal struggle with weight, is that person missing the point or getting the point? We submit that the speaker has missed the greater systemic issue surrounding race, and their account of their personal struggle with weight has effectively Whited out the point of the conversation. Weight is an important human issue, no doubt. Although there is prejudice against people of various body shapes and sizes, it does not have the same historical precedence, significance, and cumulative effect that people of color are still experiencing today because of racism.

Gentrification does not happen when lean people invade neighborhoods. You cannot disaggregate prison populations and analyze criminal behavior by people who were bullied. You cannot look at income inequality simply by studying people with divorced parents. On the other hand, some communities do have higher rates of type 2 diabetes and obesity because of a lack of

healthy food options and an overabundance of convenient and cheap processed food—not simply because of nutritional habits and diet. The root of
the inequity is in the history of race in the U.S., and is not the byproduct of
weight, size, and health.

We are focusing on a specific phenomenon that occurs within the
White architecture of the mind that ultimately defends White dominance.
Whenever a White person's story shifts the discussion away from race to topics
like weight, poverty, divorce, or even childhood trauma, it assuages the guilt
and pain of confronting systemic racism. Considering every possible source
of individual pain can obscure systemic consequences of racial injustice. This
behavior colonizes pain. It steals pain.

Lastly, there is an ongoing debate about whether or not White guilt is
useful in discussions of race and diversity. Guilt is another layer of pain. Some
contend that White guilt is fundamentally useless because its hyper-individ-
ualistic focus prevents people from seeing the larger system at work. Others
find that if guilt is the starting point for a developmental journey that leads to
greater levels of consciousness, then it can be leveraged for good.

Brené Brown highlights the difference between guilt and shame.[14] Brown
generally defines guilt as a failure that can be assessed against an individual's
set of values and standards. Discomfort can be used for growth. Shame, however, is the feeling of being deeply flawed or unworthy. Whenever we say the
word White in the context of a diversity seminar or workshop, it can change
the environment in the room. People become noticeably uncomfortable. We
believe this discomfort is related to feelings of shame in the absence of guilt.
Participants wonder why they feel so bad even though they do not feel they
have done anything wrong.

We advocate that White folks should concretely associate shame with
White systems, and that individuals should assess their guilt in ways that create consciousness around systemic impact regardless of the intent. Empathy is
not achieved by trying to connect to the actual experience someone else has
had but to the feelings and emotions behind the experience.[15] Consciousness
requires empathy in order to move away from the impulse to White-up each
other with our painful experiences. Furthermore, because of the role race has
historically played in social relationships, White pain claims should simply be
suspended when listening to accounts of racial injustice—even if the initial
instinct of the White listener is to try to connect around a shared experience.
Instead, listening, lamenting, and grieving are communal ways of holding
another's pain, in the place of making claims and stealing pain.

Notes

1. Memmi, Albert. *The Colonizer and the Colonized*. New York: Routledge, 2013.

2. Several scholars of Critical Race Theory have been instrumental in driving new research on understanding race and racism in the United States. Read the work of Delgado, Richard, and Jean Stefancic. *Critical Race Theory: The Cutting Edge*. Philadelphia: Temple University Press, 2000. Read also the work of Gloria Ladson-Billings and her colleague William Tate. Ladson-Billings, Gloria, and William F. Tate. "Toward a Critical Race Theory of Education." *Teachers College Record* 97, no. 1 (1995): 47.

3. Richard, Perez-Pena. "Rachel Dolezal Leaves N.A.A.C.P. Post as Past Discrimination Suit is Revealed," *The New York Times*, last modified June 12, 2015, http://nyti. ms/1MF2ytM.

4. Ibid.

5. Jun, Alexander, "Unintentional Racism," in *Heal Us, Emmanuel: A Call for Racial Reconciliation, Representation, and Unity in the Church*, ed. Doug Serven (Oklahoma City: Black White Bird Press, 2016), 21–26.

6. "Bernie Sanders: Black Lives Matter," *CNN Politics*, last modified October 13, 2015, http://www.cnn.com/videos/politics/2015/10/13/bernie-sanders-democratic- debate-black-lives-matter-27.cnn.

7. Smith, Daryl G. *Diversity's Promise for Higher Education: Making It Work*. Baltimore: JHU Press, 2015.

8. Crenshaw, Kimberlé. *Critical Race Theory: The Key Writings that Formed the Movement*. New York: The New Press, 1995.

9. Beauchamp, Zack. "The Real Politics behind the Covington Catholic Controversy, Explained." *Vox*. January 23, 2019. Accessed March 28, 2019. https://www.vox.com/policy-and-politics/2019/1/23/18192831/covington-catholic-maga-hat-native-american-nathan-phillips).

10. "Innocent Smirking MAGA Whiteboy Nick Sandmann." *Robert What*. April 26, 2019. Accessed June 01, 2019. https://robertwhat.com/innocent-smirking-maga-whiteboy-nick-sandmann/.

11. Coates, Ta-Nehisi. "How Stand Your Ground Relates to George Zimmerman." *The Atlantic*. July 16, 2013. Accessed March 28, 2019. https://www.theatlantic.com/national/archive/2013/07/how-stand-your-ground-relates-to-george-zimmerman/277829/.

12. "Episode 03: Misdemeanor, Meet Mr. Lawsuit—Transcript." *Serial*. Accessed April 18, 2019. https://serialpodcast.org/season-three/3/transcript.

13. "Black Girls Viewed As Less Innocent Than White Girls, Georgetown Law Research Finds." *Black Girls Viewed As Less Innocent Than White Girls, Georgetown Law Research Finds*. Accessed May 16, 2019. https://www.law.georgetown.edu/news/black-girls-viewed-as-less-innocent-than-white-girls-georgetown-law-research-finds-2/.

14. Brown, Brené. *Daring Greatly: How the Courage To Be Vulnerable Transforms the Way We Live, Love, Parent, and Lead*. New York: Penguin Books, 2012.

15. Brown, Brené. *Dare to Lead: Brave Work, Tough Conversations, Whole Hearts*. New York: Random House, 2018.

· 3 ·

WHITEFLUENZA: HOW DOMINANCE IS AN EPIDEMIC WITH NO KNOWN CURE

Twilight is a popular fiction novel series about vampires and werewolves. It is a love story in which a vampire meets an attractive young human woman, and his affection for her leads to a meet-and-greet with his vampire family—all of whom have coexisted with humans on the earth by essentially training themselves to resist feasting upon their blood. This is no small feat, as evidenced by the temptations of human flesh wafting into their presence. These well adapted vampires have re-wired their predatory instincts.

Similarly, White evolution is about the history of moving toward supremacy, and then rewriting the story for racial justice—which involves coexistence and interdependence, and training to resist and overcome the default behaviors and attitudes of dominant groups. Just like the vampires, however, no amount of resistance training for members of a dominant group can fully alleviate a thirst for power and privilege. Nevertheless, there is still tremendous value in redesigning the architecture.

Epidemiology

As parents, we (Collins and Jun) have spent our fair share of time in emergency rooms and have taken days off of work to see a primary care physician for our sick children. We bring our children in with a fever, vomiting, chills, aches and pain, and with hopeful anticipation we look to our ER doctors and pediatricians to tell us that their illness is bacterial—that it can be treated with antibiotics. Oftentimes, the doctors respond with the dreaded news: it is a virus. No known medicine can effectively cure a virus. A virus is hard to treat—it lives in the cells of our bodies and is essentially protected from medicine. The unique, protected, and complex nature of a virus makes it an apt metaphor for dominance and supremacy. White dominance is like a virus with no known cure—Whitefluenza. Notions of superiority evolve, mutate, and rapidly spread; it is very difficult to prevent or defeat.

A common virus like the flu may be painful for a short time, but it eventually passes. A more serious virus like the human immunodeficiency virus (HIV) never goes away. Other viruses can lie dormant for a decade or more, with symptoms emerging only occasionally. All components of the individual effects of viruses provide useful analogies for exploring how privilege manifests in acute and isolated cases. People who reside in positions of power exist at various stages of consciousness; they can choose to overlook dynamics of power or simply become blind to it.

However, even when individual symptoms dissipate, the virus is still alive, spreading, and mutating. As a virus replicates over time, the genes of the virus continually make small changes. As changes are made, human bodies become desensitized to the viruses that have been there all along. These mutations are genetic shifts and are why people continue to be infected by viruses even as their bodies continue to build immunities. Whitefluenza is the notion that White dominance spreads, mutates, lies dormant, is more visible at various times due to acute symptoms, and is part of a larger system where members unwittingly change the rules or perspectives to maintain dominance. At times, there may be outbreaks and even epidemics; other times, there are inoculations. During both scenarios, the systemic culture of the virus is alive and well. Similar to how the coronavirus invaded families, schools, and communities, Whitefluenza ravages through the mind of individuals and societies. It is embedded in the White architecture of the mind.

The virus spreads through the ways people speak, think, act, respond, retaliate, educate, and engage. For example, I (Collins) grew up hearing racist language outside of my home. I have family in Alabama and I grew up in Tennessee, Louisiana, Kansas, and Texas, where overt discrimination was common. This model of racism represents one strand of the virus that I knew I did not have. But because I grew up seeing and hearing this type of racism outside my home, I dealt with another strand of the virus that was harder for me to detect. Having the ability to point to something that I clearly was not (an overt bigot) veiled my ability to see my own complicity. These weaker strands of the virus are a key defender in maintaining White dominance. Inability to see the virus supports its survival and prevents inoculation in the form of recognition and consciousness.

Societies represent constructed realities, where any advantage is fiercely gripped and defended. Examples like generational wealth, bootstrap ideology, and trickle-up economics (i.e., the rich are getting richer and the poor are getting poorer) are all indications of how a belief in ownership creates a sense of protectionism. Feelings of entitlement lead to astounding resilience and dedication toward defending dominance—all of which contribute to the virus-like nature of privilege and supremacy.

Endowed Privilege

When people own material goods, they tend to overestimate their value because they are in possession of the items, whether it is a small memento or something much larger (e.g., a house). This pattern—where people demand much more to give up an object than they would be willing to pay to acquire it—is called the endowment effect[1] or status quo bias.[2] A more complex example of this idea is something called a virtual endowment, which refers to the feeling of ownership even *before* something is owned, which goes beyond just physical ownership to include attitudes, behaviors, and viewpoints. Once people experience ownership of an idea, it is difficult to let the idea go, which results in a rigid and unyielding ideology.[3] Cultures with systemic privilege and instant gratification draw mental blueprints and schemas regarding entitlements and rights. Notions of superiority are embedded within the White architecture of the mind, but are not immutable.

Endowment effects are a manifestation of an asymmetry of value. This loss aversion occurs when the disutility of giving up an object is greater than the utility associated with acquiring it. We see this phenomenon in action as individuals focus on what they may lose, rather than on what they may gain. Whenever there is uncertainty, the losses appear larger than the potential gains.[4] In a traditionally rational sense, having any kind of privilege creates a sense of endowment, and it is irrational to consider doing anything to jeopardize or even compromise that valuable asset. As a result, privilege grows and is transferred with a sense of rationality that gives it virus-like qualities.

Again, when going to a physician for a fever and congestion, patients may actually hope they have a bacterial infection, so that the doctor will write a prescription for antibiotics. However, if they have a viral infection, they will have to wait for their body to suppress the active infection instead of finding an external medical solution. A virus is a microscopic infectious agent that replicates and mutates inside of other living organisms. A healthy immune system can eliminate some viruses, and vaccines can inoculate a host from being infected. Similarly, White dominance can thrive if it is left dormant and undisturbed. Subtle manifestations of White privilege serve to maintain White dominance in a multicultural age. Since overt outbreaks draw more attention and more reaction directed at the root of the problem, the evolving virus maintains its position when it is with a host that is unaware of its existence.

Some obvious and overt instances of White supremacy in the racial history of humanity include the ability to own people of a different race, defining people of a different race as less than fully human, and preventing them from participating fully in civic affairs. These social inequities and their effects were overt and people in power fought desperately to keep them, but they could not survive the resistance movements and the emergence of Civil Rights in a multicultural age.

As a result, *overt* racism was traded in for something much easier to hide. The legal affirmation of Civil Rights and the full participation of minorities in civic life in the U.S. allowed for the argument that now everyone has an equal opportunity to succeed. Under the veneer of equal opportunity, new arguments emerged that any inequality in outcomes was rooted in personal moral failings. Family characteristics, neighborhoods, crime, income levels, drugs, and the war on drugs became new talking points about individual responsibility in a post-Civil Rights era covered by an assumption of equality. At this point, White dominance became much more like a dormant virus—it was more difficult to see, but the effects were insidious.

"Admit Your White Privilege"

Consider an interesting televised exchange between two popular media personalities. Jon Stewart, the liberal former host of The Daily Show, convinced the conservative Fox News commentator Bill O'Reilly to appear on his show in October 2014 to promote a book. Within the first moments of the conversation, Stewart said, "I have one simple goal. I want you to admit that there is such a thing as White privilege. That's all I want from you today."[5] The segment was entertaining to watch and one that is easy to find via the Internet. O'Reilly responded, "In your case, there is White privilege," but clarified that he did not actually believe that there is a thing called White privilege, and if there is, there has to be Asian privilege, "because Asians make more money than Whites." From that point, Stewart struggled to translate his rote, academic knowledge about the uniqueness and nuances of White privilege into quick, made-for-TV banter:

> So it's really—they're not equivalent. And either way, White people, males, set the system so that's what privilege is—is that White people set the system that, yes, maybe Asian immigrants want immigration policy liberalized, have done better over these past 30 or 40 years. But there has been a systemic—systemic systematized subjugation of the Black community.

If you find Stewart's words hard to read, they are also difficult to hear. He was not communicating well. It was clear he believed something different than O'Reilly, but was not able to clarify what it was. The debate moved on from the poorly explained Asian American perspective and focused on the difference between the past and the present. As O'Reilly noted, "Maybe you haven't figured out that there is no more slavery, no more Jim Crow, all right, and the most powerful man in the world is—a Black American [referring to Barack Obama]."

Stewart became more frustrated at this point and struggled to explain to O'Reilly the residual impact of "systemic subjugation." O'Reilly conceded that collectively some of this may be true, but that ultimately people still have individual choice. He told Stewart, "Listen, this is the usual White guilt liberal stuff that you guys throw out there forever." From this moment, Stewart probably made the most poignant argument in this bumpy discussion. He drew O'Reilly into an acknowledgment of how geography, neighborhoods, and upbringing leave an imprint on lives, including O'Reilly's own upbringing in Levittown, NY where his father was able to purchase a home with an affordable mortgage via the GI Bill in the 1950s. The crux of the conversation occurred when O'Reilly acknowledged that Black people could not live in his neighborhood at that time. This connection put pressure on his logic, and he reverted back to saying, "It is not that nice of a place to live," but added, "All right. If you want to say it's White privilege because Whites didn't have it as bad as Blacks, fine." O'Reilly added several other platitudes about hard work, anyone can make it, and the accusation that Stewart was ultimately pushing "victimhood."

Throughout this conversation, Stewart worked diligently, but ultimately fruitlessly, to convince or convert O'Reilly's conservative disposition. The exchange, however, provided additional layers with which to understand the concept of Whitefluenza. O'Reilly's response, of course, shows the most overt layers of privilege and denial. For some who already accept the notion of White privilege, the conservative disposition will come across as oblivious. Stewart's point about the systems built into geography and neighborhoods is valid and poignant. However, counterintuitively, the most salient point to make regarding the mutating role of the virus of Whitefluenza is less about *O'Reilly's* disposition, and more about *Stewart's*.

Whitefluenza operates in a stealthy but potent way in persons who believe they have a deep understanding of diversity in a multicultural age. Stewart is a good example. Following Stewart's show, there were plenty of accolades for Stewart and his "gotcha" moment about O'Reilly and his childhood home. There were also criticisms. When O'Reilly was leaning on aggregated pan-Asian American incomes in comparison to White incomes as proof of no White privilege unless there was Asian privilege, Stewart awkwardly tried to counter and asked, "What kind of Asians?" The author of the blog *Reappropriate*, noted, "In a world where Asian Americans make up less than 3% of those appearing even as guests on political talk shows, it's not entirely surprising that there was no Asian American (or indeed no person of color at all) to help salvage this travesty of a Whitesplaining moment."[6]

The article included a breakdown of the size of Asian American households, income contributors, and prevalence in expensive areas, which mitigate the static and linear comparison of incomes. The issue is much deeper. Privilege is not measured by income. There are nuanced factors that contribute to a system of privilege, and history is an important predictor of the future. (In fact, the article noted that Levittown, NY is still 95% White today.) In the end, there were *no* people of color on the segment. It was two White men—one struggling to articulate a position on diversity, privilege, and racial minorities, and the other denying that any concrete difference exists between White privilege and people of color.

Stewart's role in this discussion becomes more interesting in this brief case study of Whitefluenza in light of some past incidents involving writers of color on his show. For example, a 2015 *New York Times* article included an account of a dispute on the Daily Show about a racially insensitive segment.[7] A former writer on Stewart's show disclosed a heated exchange about a segment that he perceived as racially insensitive (a portrayal of a conservative Black politician). He outlined how Stewart became incensed and shouted expletives during the disagreement. The writer, who is Black, conveyed how Stewart impersonating a Black politician was "a little weird" and discouraged any repetition of the segment. Stewart shut him down— repeatedly. The argument grew in intensity and volume as the two men crossed the building to Stewart's office. Later, Stewart apologized to the staff, but the only Black writer on the show felt disrespected. When the exchange was detailed in a podcast, Stewart reached out to the writer and "kind of apologized" for "if" the writer "felt hurt," which was a hardly satisfying apology.

Stewart is liberal and actively engages in discussions of race, diversity, equity, and other issues of dominance. He is considered to be someone who understands the issues and who uses his platform to educate, inform, and advocate. However, he demonstrated inconsistencies and manifestations of Whitefluenza that are not unique to him and which raise a different challenge for White allies, something we discuss in greater detail in our chapter entitled White 22. While we are tempted to critique O'Reilly's obvious statements of privilege and denial, we must realize that Whitefluenza's infection knows no bounds. Actively utilizing a public platform for issues of racial justice does not inoculate one from the spread of Whitefluenza.

In my (Collins) own racial identity development, I have often coveted the Black pat—that is, the pat on the back from a Black person confirming my status as an ally, someone who has a greater understanding of the issues than most White people. The desire for such confirmation as a badge of honor confirms another characteristic of White dominance as a virus. It represents yet another space (social and geographic) where I can walk without fear, garner respect, and validate my status and identity. Becoming an ally adds to an already privileged endowment.

Due to the rampant denial of White supremacy in society, it is tempting to use one's acknowledgment of it as another "pat on the back." Consequently, when some people admit White privilege, they can fall into the trap of using that acknowledgment as a way to *gain* privilege, instead of continuously interrogating the role of White privilege in their interior and exterior life. The role of endowment in Whitefluenza becomes clear when you try to remove the ally badge or the Black pat from the liberal White ally. Removing a badge that validates the role of a White liberal can incite anger, rage, disappointment, resentment, and accusations of ingratitude, and unveils another side of the endowment effect. This scenario was the case in the Stewart vignette, and in my (Collins) own experience on a journey seeking validation as a White ally, while failing to recognize the opportunity to be an accomplice.

The desire for approval often leads to actions in an effort to earn or preserve the Black pat. Many have cited experiences like having a friend of color (or two), not using the n[word], openly disparaging racial prejudice when talking with a friend of color, taking a diversity class in college, attending a Black church (once), living in another country as a voluntary minority, or even adopting a child who is not White. These experiences are often employed as "evidence" of fully-attained allyship, absolving the individual of any future faux pas, or the need for continual accountability. When challenged again about their privilege, these experiences are readily available to assuage guilt or to renew credentials, leading to a renewed Black pat. Many of these experiences, however, are entirely voluntary and are accompanied by the ability to return to dominantly White spaces, including friend groups, churches, universities, neighborhoods, and country clubs. What they do not realize is that the very ability to have a choice about their involvement (what it looks like, its extent, etc.) is in itself a form of privilege, and that privilege is ever-evolving. Continued acts to earn the Black pat are like popping pills to treat the virus within. Whitefluenza is a virus that needs constant maintaining. Mitigating the symptoms does not equal a complete cure. So, when White allies are under threat of losing the power associated with being an ally, the power must evolve.

White Sponsors or White Saviors

What happens when good White people seek to do good? Do their acts of kindness and mercy remove their guilt and complicity, or has Whitefluenza simply mutated and manifested in them, in yet another version of privilege and power that feels good to the unknowing patient?

As faculty members, we guide several doctoral students in their Ph.D. dissertations. One recent dissertation focused on the role of White male administrative leaders as sponsors of Black colleagues in higher education (credit to Nathan Risdon). These White men openly discussed the manifold problems of their own efforts toward transracial sponsorship, especially with regard to the power dynamics inherent in their relationships with their protégés of color. Some confessed that sponsorship at times felt like treating emerging Black leaders as a commodity; one described sponsorship using imagery of collecting

Black protégés as trophies. This uncritical White patriarchal objectification of young Black subordinates occurs in the midst of advocacy work and ally-ship that may ultimately benefit a few visible Black leaders, but does little to change the systemic racism embedded in Dominant White Institutions.

Hart-Felt Motivations To Do Good

The story of the Hart family murder-suicide may haunt Americans for genera-tions. While the history of human society has been filled with so many restric-tions on marriage, family, religion, race, and class, the Hart family managed to break free from most of them. Historically, such restrictions were manifes-tations of narrowmindedness and were ultimately a quest for superiority and supremacy. The erasure of those restrictions can create the illusion that the original motivation for those constraints around race are also gone. In the twenty-first century, two White women can now be openly gay and married. This does not mean that discrimination against same-sex couples has been eliminated; but certainly, many of the past restrictions are gone. Furthermore, these same women may foster and adopt children to create a family, and those children can be of any race or color. There will still be opposition and hard-ship for such a family, but the legal and social restrictions have dissipated, leaving the appearance that society has finally "arrived," or at least that the current form of progress is the ultimate freedom for which we have fought.

Such was the case for Jen and Sarah Hart, who were married and living in Minnesota and ended up adopting six children (two biological sets of three siblings who were Black and multiracial). The adoptive parents were compen-sated around $2000/month for their participation in fostering and adopting children from the state of Texas.

The first set of siblings were removed from their biological mother, Tammy Scheurich, who had struggled through a rough family life, was transient for some time, and had children early in life.[8] By the time Tammy had her third child she felt as though her life was coming together. When her toddler daughter was bitten by ants and ultimately got a staph infection, her daughter was taken to the hospital, where they met a social worker from child protec-tive services. The paperwork was filled out to remove the children from her home, and Tammy, under pressure, signed a form that terminated her rights as a parent. Someone in South Texas was supposed to adopt the children, but the adoption fell through; and in 2006 the three multiracial children were taken to a White family in Minnesota. Tammy never saw or heard from the children again.

In July 2006, another set of three siblings in Texas were taken in by their aunt, who planned to adopt the children (who had been removed from their mother's house for a variety of reasons, including a drug addiction). Aunt Priscilla was on track to adopt them, but meanwhile she also had to agree that the children could not see their mother. One day, when she had allowed the mother to come and watch the children and make dinner for them, a social worker made a surprise visit. Upon finding the kids with their biological mother, the social worker told the kids to give their mother a goodbye kiss, and the mother never saw them again. A judge terminated Priscilla's opportunity to adopt the kids for allowing their mother to see them and thus violating a rule. The three Black children were taken to a White family in Minnesota where they would be in foster care.

Now the Harts were a transracial family of eight, with two White mothers and six adopted children who were Black and multiracial. On social media, the mothers shared messages about the terrible life from which the kids were taken—drugs pumping through their bodies, family members trying to disrupt the adoptions, and the *racial discrimination they faced* as a progressive multiracial family. They were upheld by their friends as the model of a heroic and open-minded family.

Hidden from the Hart's extended family and social contacts was the fact that a suspicious bruise was reported on the arm of their daughter Hannah at school, and that two months later she was removed from the elementary school to be homeschooled. In 2009, the couple was able to participate in a marriage ceremony in Connecticut, and all six children were re-enrolled in public schools. In 2010, Aunt Priscilla filed a motion to adopt her biological nieces and nephews away from the Harts, but the Texas Court of Appeals ruled against her. Later that year, one of the children was reported by the school for stealing the food of other children, and later reported to her teacher that her mother was hitting her and holding her head in cold water. Social workers and police officers found bruises on the stomach and back of the child. Another daughter was found with physical injury and told a school nurse that she was not allowed to eat very much.

In April 2011, all of the children were pulled from the elementary and middle schools to be homeschooled again. In the same month, Sarah Hart was convicted of misdemeanor domestic assault for inflicting harm to one of the daughters and was sentenced to a year of probation and community service.[9]

Over the course of 2011 and 2012, the entire family moved to Oregon, and by 2013 the Department of Human Services received an anonymous call that one of the children had been forced to lay face down on a mattress for five hours as punishment for eating leftover pizza without permission. Later that year, a doctor made note of the fact that five of the six children were significantly behind in their growth charts and recommended a caseworker attend to the family.

Over the next few years, the family became visible in viral social media moments. They attended festivals and concerts with collectives of progressive and social liberals who professed openness and compassion. At a Black Lives Matter protest, Devonte Hart was holding a sign offering free hugs, and a photo taken of him hugging a White police officer went viral. The police officer took him up on the free hug, and the up-close photo of Devonte's face in the police officer's chest reveals large tears coming from his eyes. In 2014, the photo went viral because of the immense social response to police violence against unarmed Black boys, men, and women. The photo appeared to show some hope for reconciliation. A couple of years later the family appeared in another viral moment at a Bernie Sanders' campaign rally where they had been selected to appear behind the podium. (A bird landed on the senator during his speech, which caused the video to go viral with the Hart family in the background.)

In 2017, the family moved states again, this time to Washington. Only months after being there, one of the daughters went to a neighbor's house to report being abused by her mothers. In 2018, one of the sons went to the same neighbor's house more than once a day for a week to ask for food because he was hungry. The neighbor reported the activity again, and a social worker visited the Hart house on March 23, 2018—but there was no answer. Two days later, Jen Hart drove the entire family off of a 100-foot cliff in Northern California. The deaths were ruled a murder-suicide.

Upon the discovery of the family's bodies, the unwinding of the plethora of details about their history of marriage, adoptions, abuse, movement across state lines, festivals, protests, and rallies became a fascination of the press. It is a story worth paying attention to.

No one can fully understand the motivations of Jen and Sarah Hart, but after extensive and careful analysis, it is clear that a liberal family ideal came to fruition and was embodied through two White, lesbian mothers and their six Black children. Their attendance at festivals, political rallies, and protests, as well as posts about the racism their children faced indicates that they had a lifestyle, an image, and an ideology to uphold.

Figure 3.1 is a Facebook post by Jen Hart about an encounter they had in a grocery store, where their Black son was stereotyped as an athlete. She demonstrates a combination of patience and humility as well as her presumed "woke" sensibilities by adding parenthesis about what she is really thinking during the encounter.

She wrote, "While I wanted so badly to step in and protect my son from the ongoing racial stereotyping, I didn't."[10] That particular sentiment is an interpretive key for the entire tragic event. Their self-image and outward projection were to protect and save the children from the harm their birth families and society could inflict upon them. Their lack of self-awareness

Figure 3.1: Facebook post from Jenn Hart

allowed them to inflict pain on their children, moving them from state to state to avoid facing more intense penalties, and presumably leaning on their White and perhaps even their lesbian identities to avoid being characterized as abusive parents. Their willingness to satisfy their own savior complex contributed to their ability to hurt these children. When the daily realities were difficult and did not go as planned, Jen Hart put an end to it all.

There are many elements to this family's story that indicate how Whitefluenza is a manifestation of supremacy and violence. The systemic elements include a war on drugs that penalizes Black families and a judicial system that separates children permanently from their biological families—disproportionately harming families of color. Another manifestation of an oppressive system allowed Jen and Sarah to embrace and embody a belief that their own painful experiences as lesbians ("I hurt, too") and willingness to adopt Black children overshadowed their White tendency toward racism. Furthermore, social media amplified their ability to control their image and the affirmation they received for projecting their progressiveness. And whenever a school or child protective services threatened their ability to maintain the image, they moved.

That is how Whitefluenza works. It shifts, it manifests itself in different ways, it prevents self-awareness, and it diverts a deeper understanding of reality. The deeply systemic critique that a White evolution toward racial justice and consciousness demands is a recognition of the logic and ideology that has taken Black children away from their families for hundreds of years.[11] From slavery to diagnoses of feeble-mindedness to sterilizations—and now to compassionate transracial adoptions to rescue poor Black children from unfit families and broken homes—it all plays into a history of construing Black families as unworthy and invisible; that White families alone possess the ontological and soteriological solution to the problem. Thus, a White savior complex plays into Whitefluenza, and prevents the formation of a critical racial consciousness.[12]

Shedding Whiteness

The story of Rachel Dolezal is another case of Whitefluenza evolution gone extreme and awry. Born with all of the characteristics of Whiteness, including White parents, a White community, and a White identity, Dolezal eventually grew to claim an African American identity as an adult. Her story is lengthy and continues to unfold, but some of the key elements of her case begin with the fact that her parents are White and she has brothers who are Black. Her White parents maintained that she is White, and her adopted Black brothers confirmed that she is White. One of her brothers compared her racial identity evolution to Blackface.[13] Her claims were complicated, as she avoided direct questions, maintained she did not understand questions about her race, and indicated that everyone was from the African continent. She has Black brothers, had a Black husband, has Black children, served as leader of the Spokane NAACP, and even attended a graduate program at Howard University, a historically Black institution.

The complexity of the Dolezal case emerged during her time at Howard, when she sued the university for discrimination. The Court of Appeals decision noted that she claimed discrimination based on "race" and that the university favored "African American students" over her.[14] Several psychologists who study race were quoted in news outlets as saying that this is a case of overidentification with a marginalized group and ultimately an archetype of White guilt pushed to the extreme.[15] As the story unfolded, she gained some clarity in her descriptions by admitting that she was born White but that she identifies as Black.

Using the concept of Whitefluenza, we contend that the Dolezal case is not limited to overidentification, and is ultimately something much deeper than White guilt. Rachel Dolezal's racial evolution is a choice and a symptom of an evolving Whitefluenza. The movement from suing Howard University for discrimination against being White to serving as an NAACP leader in Spokane with a Black identity represents a variation in strategies that highlight a desperation for power in diverse and multicultural spaces. It is pathological. The mutating privilege is an unconscious participant among strategies to maintain White dominance.

Confronting Disease

In order to supplement the notion of supremacy as a virus, we can also think of it more broadly as a disease. Alcoholism is recognized as a lifelong condition that is broadly categorized as a disease—even when there are no acute physical manifestations of symptoms. In a traditional recovery program, there are twelve steps: the first step is, "We admitted we were powerless over alcohol—that our lives had become unmanageable." Again, no analogy is perfectly symmetrical, but for our purposes the acknowledgment of the predisposition toward alcohol is not to surrender to the fight, but to commit to a continuous diligence.

This apt analogy demonstrates how the structure of the mind shapes daily thought processes. Counselors use the acronym SUDS to remind clients of the significance of "seemingly unimportant decisions." Even alcoholics who have been sober for thirty years without a single lapse may still have a consciousness that is predisposed to open a mental door toward alcohol. In a similar way, the White architecture of the mind has been shaped by a larger White system, and individuals are compelled to participate—even if unintentionally and unconsciously.

Colleges and universities continue to be active sites of contention around race and diversity. Returning to rhetoric generated from Fox News, in 2015, Bill O'Reilly had two guests on his show to talk about "campus madness," because the University of Vermont had a three-day retreat on White privilege, and another university brought in counselors to assist students after a confederate flag incident.[16] Mr. O'Reilly asked one of the guests if they had confronted their White privilege and they mockingly responded, "You didn't issue me a trigger warning before you asked me about my Whiteness" and then claimed to have never cashed in on White privilege. Another guest on the show noted,

> The administrators and the professors are wondering how this happened on college campuses because they're eating their own. But the professors and the administrators have created this monster through their diversity programs, through their tolerance programs which really only allowed so much tolerance and tolerate nothing at all.

The title of that segment was, "White Privilege has Infected US Elite Universities." Privilege is indeed an infection, but in this particular instance it manifests as a mockery. This mockery highlights a deep disdain for even conversing about White privilege and rejects the notion that privilege and power combine as key elements of racism. Denying the existence of a virus is a crucial component in preserving its ability to spread undetected.

Higher education is a place where transformation occurs through both retreats and protests. The conscious exploration of the virus of White supremacy will likely weaken its ability to manifest in negative ways. However, the active involvement of White allies in movements for justice and equity can still fall prey to the paradox of "help" that only hurts. The involvement of White allies does not change a White system, but can be a new manifestation of privilege that advances White dominance. Addressing the virus of supremacy is one-way individuals can begin to acknowledge and interrogate the dominant system. In the end, it is not about promoting guilt or determining whether or not someone is a bad person. The challenge is to find and dismantle unconscious or unintentional strategies that defend White dominance.

Herd Immunity and White Evolution

The public health understanding of *herd immunity* aids in explaining why vast public vaccinations help disease prevention. When there is a critical mass of people immune to disease, it benefits even those who are not immune. The key issue is critical mass. Without reaching critical mass, society is at risk. For a visual representation of herd immunity, see Figure 3.2.[17] Although families and communities who believe that vaccines are harmful will take issue with this theory, the idea behind the notion has contributed to the near eradication of deadly diseases like smallpox and measles in some regions of the world.

The concept of Whitefluenza and the accompanying examples help to cement the image that dominance and supremacy is an ever-evolving virus. There is no known cure. The question then, is what to do next. Is there any way to inoculate or evolve faster than an evolving virus? Each year doctors release a vaccination for the flu, and it is always a guess as to which strain of the flu is going to be most rampant in that particular year. Because there is no known cure, each attempt involves a certain amount of failure, but still subscribes to the theory—if enough relatively healthy people are willing to inoculate themselves, it will help the broader community.

Whitefluenza contributes to the evolution of supremacy in insidious ways—even to the extent that compassion and White efforts at being helpful should be suspect. The antidote and movement to prevent the infection (even if imperfect) is to educate for critical racial consciousness. A prerequisite for White evolution toward racial justice is a deep and ongoing commitment to the recognition that supremacy is pervasive and ever-evolving. As a result, White evolution for racial justice must also be ever-evolving toward anti-racism and critical consciousness. Commitments are often seen as individual choices, but herd immunity provides a crucial link between individual choices and public health.

Similarly, cultivating a critical racial consciousness and a commitment to an evolution for justice needs to take place at a critical mass. White

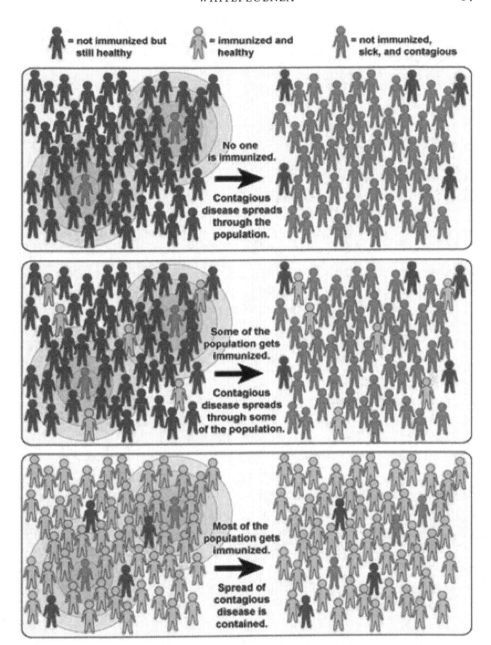

Figure 3.2: Herd immunity. Available from Wikimedia commons

supremacist ideologies—both hidden and visible—hurt all of society. From an ecological perspective, an evolution toward a critical racial consciousness should address oppression for people of color; but it is also a recognition of interdependence—our well-being is intricately connected to each other. When one segment is not doing well, neither is the other. A mere interest convergence, or pursuing the health of a neighbor for our own well-being, will not achieve consciousness or help in the fight against privilege and supremacy. Critical racial consciousness is an antidote to an education system that has been built on reinforcing the construction of inferiority and supremacy (see Chapter 8 for a deeper explanation of the concept).

Healthy people who can get vaccinated become the herd who ends up protecting the few who cannot get vaccinated for one reason or another, like newborn babies, people without immune systems, transplant patients, people without spleens, and of course those who *choose* not to get vaccinated (who thus become the weakest link in the chain). In terms of White dominance, individual inoculation is a key part of systemic change; healthy (or conscious) people help to evolve systemic White logic. White people with a relatively healthy sense of racial identity must recognize that their regular vaccinations make them the herd; they then serve to protect the weak—meaning those who are anemic when it comes to understanding that systemic racism exists. People who are actively racist, attend alt-right rallies, and deny racial profiling of Black citizens, or who respond to "Black Lives Matter!" with "White Lives Matter!" represent a more active part of the virus.

Under the herd immunity analogy, not everyone will get the vaccine. White evolution is the acknowledgment that racism is a permanent fixture, even while it is a movement toward critical racial consciousness. The structural change may ultimately come through herd immunity—an attempt to achieve critical mass consciousness. But this would mean that enough White people must acknowledge supremacy and evolve in a diverse community where the burden of evolution is no longer solely on the backs of people of color.

In conclusion, we submit that it is critical to remain both aware of and vigilant about the various forms of dominance that exist in all of us. Furthermore, we must recognize and admit to our inability to fully rid ourselves of the benefits of privilege that we enjoy. Once we have tasted it and benefited from power, we are deeply reluctant to let it go. When we deny the existence of a virus and fail to address it, we make a crucial error that leads to unwittingly allowing it to infiltrate a system and to spread and mutate while remaining undetected. However, addressing the virus of power, actively engaging in prevention and intervention, frequent self-examinations, and regular check-ups with experts will help both White people and people of color move toward the evolution of racial consciousness.

Notes

1. Samuelson, William, and Richard Zeckhauser. "Status Quo Bias in Decision Making." *Journal of Risk and Uncertainty* 1, no. 1 (1988): 7–59.
2. Thaler, Richard. "Toward a Positive Theory of Consumer Choice." *Journal of Economic Behavior & Organization* 1, no. 1 (1980): 39–60.
3. Schwartz, Hugh. "Predictably Irrational: The Hidden Forces that Shape Our Decisions." *Business Economics* 43, no. 4 (2008): 69–72.
4. Kahneman, Daniel, and Amos Tversky. "Choices, Values, and Frames." *American Psychologist* 39, no. 4 (1984): 341.
5. Taibi, Catherine, "Jon Stewart Tries to Make Bill O'Reilly Admit White Privilege Exists. And Fails," *Huffington Post*, last modified October 16, 2014, http://www. huffingtonpost. com/2014/10/16/jon-stewart-bill-oreilly-white-privilege-daily- show_n_5995726.html.
6. "How Both Bill O'Reilly and Jon Stewart Got It Really Wrong on Asian Americans," *Reappropriate*, last modified October 16, 2014, http://reappropriate.co/2014/10/ how-both-bill-oreilly-and-jon-stewart-got-it-really-wrong-on-asian-privilege/.
7. Itzkoff, Dave, "Daily Show' Writer Recalls Heated Dispute with Jon Stewart," *The New York Times*, last modified July 24, 2015, http://www.nytimes.com/2015/07/25/ arts/ television/daily-show-writer-recalls-heated-dispute-with-jon-stewart.html.
8. "A Mother Grapples With an Adoption That Led to Deaths." *The Appeal*. Accessed March 28, 2019. https://theappeal.org/hart-family-fatal-crash-birth-mother-scheurich/.
9. For a comprehensive review of the story see the podcast and supplementary documents in the podcast entitled Broken Harts. Glamour. "'Broken Harts': A Timeline." *Glamour*. March 12, 2019. Accessed March 28, 2019. https://www.glamour.com/story/ broken-harts-timeline.
10. "Hart Family Crash—A Collection of Screenshots of Jen Hart's Facebook Posts." *Reddit*. Accessed March 28, 2019. https://www.reddit.com/r/hartfamilycrash/comments/ ah35sl/a_collection_of_screenshots_of_jen_harts_facebook/.
11. Eberhardt, Jaz. "160 Years, Part III: Black History and the Invisible Children." *The Record*. February 22, 2019. Accessed March 28, 2019. https://buffstaterecord.com/13408/ culture/160-years-part-iii-black-history-and-the-invisible-children/.
12. Jun, Alexander, Tabatha L. Jones Jolivet, Allison N. Ash, and Christopher S. Collins. *White Jesus: The Architecture of Racism in Religion and Education*. New York: Peter Lang Publishing New York, 2018.
13. Moyer, Justin, "'Are You an African American?' Why an NAACP Official Isn't Say-ing." *The Washington Post*, last modified June 12, 2015, https://www.washington post.com/news/ morning-mix/wp/2015/06/12/spokane-naacp-president- rachel-dolezal-may-be-white/.

14. "NAACP Imposter Sued School Over Race Claims," *The Smoking Gun*, last modified June 15, 2015, http://www.thesmokinggun.com/documents/bizarre/rachel- dolezal-discrimination-lawsuit-786451.

15. Thompson, Krissah, "Rachel Dolezal: What the Rights Activist's Story Says about Being White in Modern America," *The Independent*, last modified June 15, 2015, http:// www.independent.co.uk/news/world/americas/rachel-dolezal-what-the- rights-activists-story-says-about-being-white-in-modern-america-10318082.html.

16. This segment of the O'Reilly Factor aired on the Fox News network on December 1, 2015.

17. "What Is Herd Immunity?" *PBS*. Accessed March 28, 2019. https://www.pbs.org/wgbh/nova/article/herd-immunity/.

· 4 ·

WHITE 22: WHITE IF YOU DO, WHITE IF YOU DON'T

The concept of White 22 is based on the presupposition that racial dialogues are a trap. No matter what you do, you are going to be wrong—especially if you are White. Through online outlets, a variation of Figure 4.1 was posted to advance the idea that the only conclusion of racial considerations is to identify a White person as racist. The concept is a polemic one, driving at the supposed futility of racial considerations. The underlying message is that if you are White, you are unworthy and unredeemable, no matter what positive effort you exhibit. The logic of this argument and defense mechanism is demonstrated in Figure 4.1 You are White if you do, and White if you don't. If this is the logical conclusion of any diversity conversation, then why would anyone be willingly subjected to the abuse? The logic of White 22 serves as a sign of caution about getting involved in such discussions at all.

In the wake of Michael Brown's death in Ferguson, MO in 2014, individuals and groups of people gathered to protest the shooting of another unarmed Black man. Religious groups got involved, grassroots activism emerged, and the scenes of protest persisted as the decision on whether or not to indict the officer continued to drag out. We heard of a progressive White woman who felt compelled to travel to Ferguson to join the protest and be in solidarity. She wanted to join her Black brothers and sisters because of her concern for

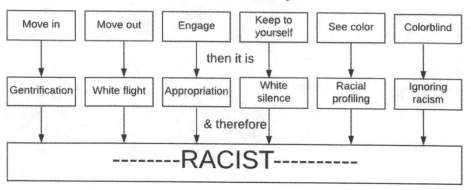

Figure 4.1: White 22 logic

racial justice. To her dismay, rather than receiving the coveted Black pat for showing up and for being a good White person, she was challenged by several Black protesters as to her motivation for being present, as she was yelling and screaming and attempting to link arms. They asked her, "What are you doing here?" It came as a surprise to the woman and became a real predicament in terms of trying to figure out what to do next. She had spent time and money to travel across the country. She had made her way to an intensely emotional scene—the heart of a struggle for justice—and was immediately challenged. Perhaps some White readers can relate to being shut down by colleagues and friends of color in what White people have misunderstood to be critical moments of solidarity. Undoubtedly there are other examples at similar rallies and protests across the nation. This chapter covers the contradictions in White involvement whenever White people opt in to a struggle for racial equity and justice. Where do White people fit in when it comes to discussions and actions on racial consciousness? Where do White people find the right disposition in a racial dialogue and what might one's disposition be? Cultural humility can only be developed in community. White 22 exposes the fallacy that any individual can grow in consciousness absent a community, but also addresses the dangers of burdening communities of color to teach White enlightenment.

One blog was entitled, "Dear White People: Ferguson Protests are a Wake, Not a Pep Rally," and included poignant reflections about the pain of feeling ontologically isolated and denied through the national events and media coverage. The author recalled attending protests and noted,

[W]hite "allies" come out to support the cause, yet struggle to feel comfortable surrounded by Black people and so clump with their friends, take pictures to prove that they were there and subtly and unconsciously fight to control the space with their chants. Often, this fight for control is more obvious, like white people taking the mic and talking about why they are there.[1]

The author acknowledged that the problem is subtle, but as tragedies become momentary opportunities and moments become movements, the subtle problems are magnified. In contrast to the behavior of White allies, the author noted that

[f]or many Black people, Ferguson protest [sic] are not a public pep rally for racial unity, they are a living wake. We are dying. We are being killed by the police. We are getting lynched by the media. Our souls are nearly suffocating by the pressure of being a problem.[2]

What is the role for White people in these spaces and movements? What constitutes suitable behavior and consciousness? When it comes to being White in diverse spaces, a no-win or Catch-22 (in reference to Joseph Heller's best-selling book) attitude has evolved. There is a tension between the notion that inaction is an injustice and a threat to justice, and the sentiment that "this is not my struggle, so I won't get involved."

Straight White Men

The play, *Straight White Men*, went through a unique process to develop the main character.[3] The playwright held a position in residence at Brown University where community members from various identity groups provided input for the White character they wanted to see in the performance. The sentiments were summarized by the desire for a character that would sit down, shut up, and listen. Upon the formation and presentation of the character, the same audience who helped develop the play in fact hated the character when he appeared in the performance. His uber-passive nature did not appeal to the very people who wanted to see those characteristics in action. The playwright, Young Jean Lee, called the task of writing the straight White male character an existential dilemma. This dilemma is a White 22—the futility that White people feel when they are criticized or challenged while engaged in racial justice.

At the beginning of the drama, the White, liberal family at the center of the story is gathered around a gameboard that adapted Monopoly into a new game called "Privilege." One brother pulls what is called an "excuse card." The other brother, the main character in the play, reads the card dryly: "What I just said wasn't racist/sexist/homophobic because I was joking ... Pay $50 to an LGBT organization."[4] The brief scene in the play illustrates the sense of futility that White people may feel when criticized or challenged while engaging in racial justice.

Any individual caught in what they perceive as a no-win situation will be frustrated. White 22 carries with it some natural elements of resentment, confusion, and exasperation. I (Collins) found myself frustrated at times during my own White racial identity development. A fundamental dilemma occurs when someone with White privilege has a moment of clarity and tries to break through the privilege to advocate for justice and is later rejected or criticized. The previous vignette about the White woman who joined the Ferguson protest is akin to this example. The refrain that sometimes emerges at this moment is, "I tried to help you all." Embedded in this sentiment is a root problem, often called the White knight or White savior syndrome. What feels like White 22 is ultimately the assumed ownership of helpful expertise or energy resulting in paternalism that only serves to recreate problems. Critical race theorists disparage White involvement using the term *interest convergence* to point out that White folks get involved when there is some reciprocal benefit—such as the feeling of doing something savior-like, or gaining access to another social setting where they are deemed acceptable.[5] White 22 and the frustrating acknowledgment of one's inability to "do anything right" when it comes to racial justice actually reveals a subtle version of White dominance.

When the Desire to Help Hurts

A book focused on poverty reduction is entitled *When Helping Hurts*. It explores how efforts from religiously affiliated mission organizations try to help low-income communities, but often inadvertently cause harm. Efforts to help often come with a subtle and unconscious messianic air of superiority, which has evolved in the economically wealthy through a fundamental belief in their own hard work.[6] The premise of the book is that flawed poverty alleviation exacerbates not only the economic poverty of the poor, through feelings of inferiority and shame, but also the "poverty of being" found in a false sense of superiority based on wealth.

Similarly, when anyone in a dominant group attempts to deal with privilege and gets involved in diversity and justice work, the attempt to help can hurt and exacerbate the issue. It is White 22. Claims of compassion fatigue, of trying but of not being accepted, feeling paralyzed, and saying "it doesn't matter what I do" are all ways in which White 22 actually becomes another strategy for maintaining White dominance. The notion of attempting to help, being rejected, feeling trapped, and avoiding the internal and conscious-ness-raising work required exacerbates a deeply rooted dominant White sys-tem. Approaching diversity work with good intentions can clearly lead to a "when helping hurts" phenomenon.

Moreover, the very notion of a "helping hurts" critique will lead some White people to feel frustrated and want to give up. Robin Di Angelo writes about what she terms White fragility, a corollary construct that helps inform White 22 and vice versa. According to Di Angelo,

> On the rare occasion that our worldviews, positions or entitlement are questioned, it throws us so off balance that we basically lose our minds. We become outraged, hurt, offended and so on, and push back with a range of defensive moves (cry, argue, withdraw, refuse to engage). These moves function to end the challenge and get us back on our racial footing.[7]

Whenever we hear White colleagues express frustration because they cannot win, we are reminded that the premise of winning is itself problematic. There is no way for victories to be won when it comes to racialized pain, and the sooner friends in White dominant positions recognize this, the sooner they will be able to temper their expectations and embrace the realities that their friends of color have long understood when it comes to systemic racism: it is a long arduous struggle that no one individual could ever resolve alone.

The concept of "when helping hurts" extends further into the psychol-ogy of alleviating a global problem like poverty. The notion extends into the development industry that has accompanied the construction of global inequality. Development discourse supports the idea that Africa and the Southern Hemisphere need Northern and Western interventions.[8] It centers the White "west" in relation to the needs of the "rest" who have been *othered* by middle-class White Northern knowledge systems and values.

Barbara Heron's book *Desire for Development* provides a theoretical building block in one's recognition that White bourgeois identity formation includes a person thinking of herself as a moral agent. The book excavates the notion of desire and the longing for Whiteness, which carries the prom-ise of wholeness. Examining systemic Whiteness on this global scale, where Canadian women (in the case of Heron's book) exhibit a strong desire to

help, unveils the age-old driving desire to be in the right, to be "okay," innocent, and without blame. White guilt plays a role in this phenomenon as well.
Wherever guilt exists, it must be alleviated. To be White is to be alright, and
if there is evidence of wrongdoing then White innocence is in question. As
a result, Heron claims, the desire for development (or in our case, the desire
for diversity) is again about the moral compass for the maintained dominance
of the White system. Claiming that an attempt was made and it is a no-win
situation supports the current system and becomes a barrier to deeper layers
of consciousness.

Given the reality of intersectionality of identity for White women (i.e.,
gender, sexual orientation, class), it is interesting to note how this group
intentionally and unintentionally hinders the progress of racial justice. While
the role and impact of some White women in the movement toward gender
equality is clear, their role in racial equity can get complicated sometimes—
and is not often addressed in anti-racism literature. Frances Kendall's book
on privilege is an exception, with an excellent chapter on this issue of how
White women perpetuate White supremacy.[9]

Similar to Heron's and Kendall's excavation of White women's contribution to the problem, Lori Patton and Stephanie Bondi conducted a study on
White men who were perceived to be in support of diversity and equity movements in higher education. Entitled *Nice White Men or Social Justice Allies*, the
primary issue discussed was how do these men construe their role and navigate the complexities of it?[10] Central to the background of the study was the
primary understanding of an ally as someone who is working toward justice
from a dominant position (e.g., a straight person in support of gay and lesbian
people). Dominant group membership is a prerequisite for being an ally, and
in the case of White allies, one author noted, "The desire to be and be known
as a good white person stems from the recognition that our whiteness is problematic, a recognition that we try to escape by being demonstrably different
from other, racist whites."[11]

Patton and Bondi argue that White men have the most to lose in the pursuit of racial justice. This may be true in some instances, but they also profit by
gaining the ability to navigate a new social space. As we noted in our chapter
on Whitefluenza, "[t]he very acknowledgment of our racism and privilege can
be turned to our advantage."[12] They also make the point that although some
White men have experienced oppression related to socioeconomic status or
being gay, their Whiteness and maleness afford them more ability to negotiate
and surpass the obstacles. Participants in the study worked to help individuals

in difficult situations, remove systemic barriers like standardized test scores, and performed other actions that they found to be personally meaningful. Ultimately the authors of the study found that the participants were engaged more in "nice guy" activities that ultimately did not challenge the core of the system. The authors encouraged people who identify with the participants to continue wrestling with the question, "What right do I have to do this work?" and to think about it institutionally and systemically, not just individually. For those still focused on individuality and seeking personal fulfillment in racial justice, the South African concept of *ubuntu*, (the concept of human interdependence: I am not fully human until *you* are fully human) is a profound reminder of the truncated way individualism shapes our relationships and behavior.

The idea of being stuck or paralyzed is also part of a widespread notion of White racial identity development, which was articulated by Janet Helms.[13] When one feels the immobility of White 22, the temptation is to give up any more attempts at racial identity development in favor of a more inactive, isolated, and disinterested state. Part of the development, however, is overcoming racist attitudes or behaviors, which are assumed to exist in everyone. There is a well-developed body of literature that is built upon the belief that White persons should move through stages of identity development that progress from ignorance and colorblindness to an increasing recognition of Whiteness and working through guilt, to becoming an autonomous and racially aware being. One study argued that most university campuses are safe and comfortable White spaces that actually foster racial arrested development, which serves to continue to reproduce existing hierarchies.[14] Our point is also that the stagnation associated with White 22 supports White dominance. Instead of succumbing to paralysis, we must be moving through the stages, breaking down our own ignorance and biases, and constantly pursuing a robust racial identity in an active and communal context. This is no easy task, but it is vital in disrupting the systems of White dominance in ourselves and our environments.

When anti-racism instructors try to dislodge the paralysis of White 22 within their White audience, a return to the fortified safety of pain claims is typical (see Chapter 2, White Pain). This makes intergroup dialogues difficult, because White people (most notably university students) tend to claim the same disenfranchised status as students of color and other marginalized groups. It is ironic to hear a White participant criticize victimhood and simultaneously claim victim status in a moment of White theatricality.

Nolan Cabrera and other authors advocate that in order to prevent White racial arrested development, intergroup dialogues must facilitate and embrace discomfort.[15] Individual discomfort should also point to systemic questions, so that issues of race are not seen as completely personal. The notion of feeling caught in a White 22 is akin to White racial arrested development. It is necessary to understand the connection between White 22 and White Pain in order to take on the challenge of addressing these systemic issues.

When to Sit Down—The Speech Heard 'Round the Internet

In June 2016, the multiracial actor, Jesse Williams, accepted the humanitarian award from BET (Black Entertainment Television). His acceptance speech was an instantaneously viral and invigorating challenge. It is worth quoting at length here:

> There has been no war that we have not fought and died on the front lines of. There has been no job we haven't done. There is no tax they haven't levied against us—and we've paid all of them. But freedom is somehow always conditional here. "You're free," they keep telling us … Now, freedom is always coming in the hereafter, but you know what, though, the hereafter is a hustle. We want it now. And let's get a couple things straight, just a little side note—the burden of the brutalized is not to comfort the bystander. That's not our job, alright—stop with all that. If you have a critique for the resistance, for our resistance, then you better have an established record of critique of our oppression. If you have no interest, if you have no interest in equal rights for black people then do not make suggestions to those who do. Sit down.
>
> We've been floating this country on credit for centuries, yo, and we're done watching and waiting while this invention called whiteness uses and abuses us, burying black people out of sight and out of mind while extracting our culture, our dollars, our entertainment like oil—black gold, ghettoizing and demeaning our creations then stealing them, gentrifying our genius and then trying us on like costumes before discarding our bodies like rinds of strange fruit. The thing is though … the thing is that just because we're magic doesn't mean we're not real.[16]

The video of the acceptance speech was covered by every major news outlet and went viral on social media. The response to the acceptance speech was divided. On one side many people felt Williams had articulated critical points from a valuable platform. On the other side were White responses that represent the concept of White 22. Justin Timberlake was one of millions of viewers watching, and he tweeted that he was inspired. Another Twitter user responded, "So does this mean you're going to stop appropriating our music and culture?" to which Timberlake replied, "Oh, you sweet soul. The more you realize that we are the same, the more we can have a conversation. Bye." The response ignited a plethora of comments to Timberlake, including photos of him in cornrows, wave caps, and other images used to indicate his appropriation of Black culture. Three hours after the original post and the hundreds of comments that followed, Timberlake tweeted that he felt "misunderstood" and "I really do feel that we are all one ... A human race."[17]

Timberlake got White 22ed. The Williams speech was a moment of clarity and even revelry, as BET attendees stood before the speech was over and online postings multiplied at a rapid pace. Timberlake's involvement and eventual apologizing to "anyone that felt I was out of turn" shifted the focus back to the complexity of White association and involvement, which manifests in appropriation. His lackluster apology pushed the White 22 moment through cycles of colorblindness, rejection, and White guilt.

Conservative commentator Tomi Lahren delivered a more overt articulation of resistance to the acceptance speech. Embedded in her critique were a few highlights of what have become classically White responses to revolutionary thought. Lahren said:

> Well, the BET awards were last night, notably they were very Black. Oh! But can I say that, what with my Whiteness and all? Well too damn bad! Question—Was this a celebration of Black entertainment or an opportunity to complain about the plight of wealthy Black actors and musicians? Curious, because I saw a lot of talent on that stage but at the same time, a whole lot of victimhood. Oh, and police bashing, that too ...
>
> Equal Rights? Please tell me, Mr. Williams, what rights Black people don't have? Also, White people? We do, in fact, have a record of critique of your oppression! In fact, do you know how many of our ancestors fought in the Civil War to free your ancestors? Bloodiest war in the United States history was over what was right and it was largely White people fighting in it. In fact it was White Southern Democrats who fought for, not against slavery ... I'm sorry, Jesse, but I won't be apologizing for my Whiteness, just as you don't need to apologize for your Blackness! It's not White people working to divide America! It's you![18]

Several popular media personalities make a living by designing overt responses to viral events or messages. In this case, Lahren's rhetoric taps into notions of (a) boundaries about what White people can or cannot say; (b) wealthy Black people, which is presumed to undercut any message or claims about systemic racism; (c) protesting police violence, which is equated with unfairly attacking the police; (d) the role of White people in the Civil War as the heroes; and (e) that people of color are a problem because they keep talking about diversity.

If Williams' message had not been so widely distributed through social media and other outlets, it would never have garnered the attention of commentators. The message censured the naysayers who advocated that there is nothing race-based about the division of benefits in the United States. The bimodal White response was a weak and shallow message of solidarity on one side and complete rejection and mockery on the other side. In the end, both responses are stuck in a mire of White 22—you are White if you agree, and White if you disagree. Williams' comment that those who critique resistance without critiquing oppression should "sit down" also reflects the difficulty in writing the play *Straight White Men*, mentioned earlier. Claiming paralysis is synonymous with saying there is nothing to be done, especially because "you will not approve of me no matter what I do." This then becomes the rationale to do nothing; to remain silent. We introduce the concept of White silence in Chapter 7. Taking the position that there is nothing to be done serves to maintain the existing White dominant structure.

There is a de facto paralysis, and there is in fact much work for folks in a dominant group to do; but the first step is to sit down. Be quick to listen more, and slow to speak. Be prepared to be a little uncomfortable. Allow critical consciousness to uproot the White architecture of the mind that leads to a defensive posture. Be slow to respond defensively to every challenge toward your efforts of solidarity.

Admissions and Confessions

In 2018, we attended the American Educational Research Association conference and had a book signing with Peter Lang Publishing for the predecessor to this book, *White Out*. As professors of higher education, we took the opportunity to attend the off-Broadway play by Josh Harmon entitled *Admissions*. The play had been reviewed by the major news outlets in higher education and we arrived early to secure our spots in an intimate house that had fewer than 300 seats. It was almost uncomfortable before the play started because everyone knew the play was about race and college admissions—and almost everyone in the theater was White. This was also a full year before the 2019 "Varsity Blues" college admissions scandal, where a number of famous actors, actresses, and other wealthy people paid tremendous amounts of money to falsify testing scores and athletic records, with the ultimate goal of sneaking their children into selective institutions through a trapdoor (Figure 4.2).

The setting of the play is in the kitchen and living room of a White family who works at a selective and dominantly White private high school where the mother, Roberta, has worked tirelessly to diversify the school. Her explanations of the necessity of including people of color in the view book and the importance of equity, diversity, and inclusion are presented almost as caricatures of liberal White self-importance. When Roberta says diversity is important, the subtext is that it is important because she decided it is important. The author certainly moves the audience into fits of nervous laughter, cathartic laughter, and guilt-ridden silence. One critical reviewer wrote:

> In the first half of Harmon's show, we're being pushed to let our Secret Racist flags fly ("admissions" also means "confessions"), and in the second half we are, like Roberta, being taken to task. It's a strangely religious structure: Confession and Repentance. Serving as maestro of this tonal shift—and Harmon's voice-of-the-playwright character—is Sherri's 17-year-old son Charlie.[19]

Figure 4.2: Photo of Authors in New York at the play, *Admissions*

Charlie embodies White 22 in a powerfully theatrical manner. He is the son of liberal, diversity-minded parents, but ultimately serves as a mirror to their inadequacies in racial reasoning.

The climax of the story comes when Charlie finds out that he has not been accepted by Yale, but his multiracial friend, Perry, has. Perry is the son of a White mother and multiracial father, who also work at the private school. This is the moment that pent up White logic systems have been waiting for—the hypocrisy of racial reasoning is revealed on the stage, and it is cathartic. Charlie says:

> Is Penélope Cruz a person of color? Is Kim Kardashian? If so, why isn't, say, Marion Cotillard? And why does Perry's mother act as if "it's this huge achievement that a not totally white baby popped out of her vagina"? Should white people hate white people?[20]

It is mesmerizing to watch the show with an audience that is enjoying this logical conundrum with a sense of anticipation and fear. White people constructed systems of race whereby they gained centuries of privilege, but now that it has been exposed and deconstructed in the pursuit of diversity while race (as a proxy) is attacked. So, the character Charlie is ranting to his parents and reaches a point of total exasperation as he pours out his emotions to them:

> I am drowning over here, okay? ... I'm not an idiot, I don't have white pride, but I don't *hate* myself ... And by the way, who even decides? 'Cause I would really like to meet the person who decides who counts as a person of color and who doesn't ... 'Cause my mom's dad had to escape before like half his family was murdered by Nazis, but now when we all apply to college, I go in the shit pile ... [because]—shocker!—they found a new way to keep Jews out: They just made us white instead, and the grandsons of Nazis who came to America go in the exact same pile as me, which makes absolutely no sense .... But keep pushing me, keep fucking pushing me ... tell me how white I am and how disgusting I am, I'll just stand in the corner taking it all in until I can't fucking take it anymore and I all of a sudden break out into a FUCKING SIEG HEIL![21]

It is not just race that he attacks; he also criticizes the woman who earned an editor position at the school (because she is a woman) and a classmate who wanted more writers of color included in the curriculum. Charlie is in pain, but ultimately represents a cathartic White admission: he captures the frustration and hypocrisy bound up in White 22. Despite the exposure of the fallacies and inadequacies in racial reasoning, Charlie's logic does not have moral authority. His White pain does not justify the pervasive ignoring of pressing racial realities in light of his waitlisted status. White 22 is yet another tool used to justify White pain. To the playwright's credit, Charlie's father calls him an "over-privileged brat" and "racist spoiled little shit." With an audience full of White folks, a White cast, and a White playwright, there are lots of important architectures on display when watching this show.

Beware of Heroes and Allies

There are many critiques to racial reasoning, one of which is the idea that it is a conspiracy theory founded on untruth, fake news, and a victim mentality by people of color. This conspiracy theory critique is one that tries to discredit explanations about our social realities through a racial lens. By calling it a conspiracy theory, all of its explanations are labeled as manufactured. There is no need to dismantle a racist system if the whole concept of systemic racism is fictitious.

But consider the concept of the *hidden hand* in economics as a way to convey that there is a system that coordinates the movement of a variety of monetary factors to make society work. If there is a collection of unseen forces that move value, supply, demand, and wealth around, and this unseen force is an acceptable explanation of the cash flows that are a cornerstone of how everything on our modern earth operates, why is it so difficult to accept that supremacy and racism exist on a systemic level too? There is a hidden hand of White supremacy. If we only named that term, it may seem nothing more than another facet of a grand conspiracy theory. But when compared to a fundamental theory in our understanding of how contemporary society works, perhaps it is more viable. Understanding the hidden hand of White supremacy is an important factor in processing White 22.

Consider an example from World War II. According to the history books and cultural accounts of the war, who was evil? The answer is almost universally Hitler, the Nazis, and anti-Semitism. Conversely, who was a hero? Anyone who fought them—primarily the United Kingdom, led by Winston Churchill who was an untamable lion of a leader. He was just the right combination of tenacious and uncouth to tackle the greatest evil the world had ever seen.

The War was a quagmire for determining right moral action. The grandiose nature of ethnic cleansing in the holocaust led pacifist Christian traditions to surrender their principles for the sword. The leader of the fight against Nazi Germany was the United Kingdom, but one group that suffered immense loss in this war is often concealed in historical accounts and recollections. The most extensive part of the tragedy is the five million Jews and another five million victims at the hands of the Nazis. However, another group also suffered extensive loss of life.

The U.S. lost just over 400,000, and the U.K. lost about 450,000. Japan, the other imperial aggressor, lost almost three million people to atomic bombs—an extraordinary loss of life. The action in WWII spread throughout East Asia, the pacific, and Europe. Both the Russians and the Chinese lost tens of millions of lives, but one English colony, India, where not one battle took place, had a profound death rate.

This colony had to send soldiers and supplies to England for the war, but they only suffered 87,000 military deaths. The other millions of lives lost came in a different form. Once Japan occupied Burma, the English got nervous because India imported a lot of rice from this country. So, they used a scorched-earth strategy, burning any rice fields and potential resources that could have been useful and attractive to Japan, thus destroying the northeastern part of India. This began the great famine of 1943. In spite of fervent pleas for help, no assistance was provided to the British colony of India. The justification was that all resources had to be focused on the war. But India was the source of many supplies, so this policy did not quite make sense. In the end, journalist Madhusree Mukherjee is quoted as writing, it was "not so much racism as the imbalance of power inherent in the social Darwinian pyramid that explains why famine could be tolerated in India while bread rationing was regarded as an intolerable deprivation in wartime Britain."[22] We disagree—White supremacy drove the imbalance of power.

Around the same time, Gandhi launched a movement of peaceful resistance. Churchill, considered a heroic leader, said that Gandhi "ought to be lain bound hand and foot at the gates of Delhi, and then trampled on by an enormous elephant with the new Viceroy seated on its back." When the peace movement grew, Churchill added: "I hate Indians. They are a beastly people with a beastly religion." And in order to justify the absence of any relief for the famine caused by his government's harsh actions, he suggested it was the Indians' own fault for breeding like rabbits.[23] Clearly, racism is not a simplistic evil in the hearts of few. It was the only way the system of power could be maintained in favor of the already powerful. People of color were so dehumanized by racism that hypocritical oppression became justified, even necessary, for "the greater good," the benefit of the White man. Racism is a survival strategy of systemic power:

When a large proportion of the population votes for politicians and political efforts that explicitly use racism as a campaigning tool, we tell ourselves that such huge sections of the electorate simply cannot be racist, as that would render them heartless monsters. But this isn't about good and bad people. The covert nature of structural racism is difficult to hold to account.[24]

There is not so much a conspiracy in the shadows as much as there is a structure that benefits people who are White, live in White spaces, and work in dominantly White institutions. You do not have to be an evil person to accept the benefits of that structure. When someone is called a hero or an ally, what does that say about the structure? George W. Bush accepted a bust of Churchill from the British government and upon accepting it commented, "He was a man of great courage. He knew what he believed. And he really kind of went after it in a way that seemed like a Texan to me." The President explained why he planned to display the likeness of an Englishman inside the Oval Office: "He charged ahead, and the world is better for it."[25]

Most history books would agree. But what about the families, descendants, and communities of Bengal that lost three million people to an unnecessary famine purposefully set by the British government? There is a structure to dominance and a hidden hand of White supremacy at work. Brown-skinned families were deliberately tortured by hunger and ultimately destroyed in order to maintain the power of the White colonizers. This was not an individual decision, but a systemic one. Where White 22 focuses on the personal dilemma of one's actions and inactions, a better understanding of racism sees the systemic nature of racism and one's place in it. While White supremacy is not merely personal and local, it is more systemic and global with a long history. This is why resisting racism goes way beyond a commitment to not use a racial slur. We must acknowledge the systemic nature of racism and work to dismantle it in a communal way.

Evolving Out of the Trope of White 22

The White logic that leads back to tropes of no-win solutions, White victimization, and the quest for heroes without critical consciousness prevents evolution and growth. White guilt is not useful. To embrace White guilt is to claim that no matter what you do, it will never be enough—it is embracing a nihilistic approach to racial consciousness.

The paradox of White 22 is that it is actually not a threat to the White individual, since it ultimately preserves White dominance when the White ally abandons the anti-racism field in discouragement. But White 22 is a threat to people of color who encounter White allies who have not fully examined the potential violence of their desire to help and to save those around them. The very medicine offered is then a poisonous dose without context, consciousness, and a commitment to a critical evolution toward racial justice. White 22 single-handedly reaffirms White dominance while absolving one of responsibilities in the fight against racism. It is a dangerous tool in the arsenal of White supremacy that continues to maintain the structures already in place.

Notes

1. Goggans, Aaron, "Dear White People: Ferguson Protests Are a Wake Not a Pep Rally," last modified November 26, 2014, https://wellexaminedlife.com/2014/11/26/dear-white-people-ferguson-protests-are-a-wake-not-a-pep-rally/.
2. Ibid.
3. Ulaby, Neda, "Straight White Men," A Play Explores the Reality of Privilege, last modified November 17, 2014, http://www.npr.org/sections/codeswitch/2014/11/17/364760889/in-straight-white-men-a-play-explores-the-reality-of-privilege.
4. Ibid.
5. Taylor, Edward. "A Primer on Critical Race Theory: Who Are the Critical Race Theorists and What Are They Saying?" *The Journal of Blacks in Higher Education* 19 (1998): 122.
6. Corbett, Steve, and Brian Fikkert. *When Helping Hurts: How to Alleviate Poverty Without Hurting the Poor … and Yourself.* Chicago: Moody Publishers, 2014.
7. Di Angelo, Robin, "White Liberal Racism: An Interview with Dr. Robin Di Angelo," *The Huffington Post*, last updated on August 18, 2016, http://www.huffingtonpost.com/carol-smaldino/white-liberal-racism-an-i_b_11565484.html.See also, Di Angelo, Robin. "White Fragility." *The International Journal of Critical Pedagogy* 3, no. 3 (2011).
8. Heron, Barbara. *Desire for Development: Whiteness, Gender, and the Helping Imperative.* Waterloo, Ontario: Wilfrid Laurier University Press, 2007. We find this book to be essential reading. It follows the recollections of White Canadian women who engaged in development work across the continent of Africa. Heron revealed how desire and identity is intertwined with race, class, and gender. There is a deep desire to be situated as doing good in the world, a desire which requires another to, in fact, be in need of help.
9. Kendall, Frances. *Understanding White Privilege: Creating Pathways to Authentic Relationships Across Race.* New York: Routledge, 2012.
10. Patton, Lori D., and Stephanie Bondi. "Nice White Men or Social Justice Allies?: Using Critical Race Theory to Examine How White Male Faculty and Administrators Engage in Ally Work." *Race Ethnicity and Education* 18, no. 4 (2015): 488–514.

11. Thompson, Audrey. "Tiffany, Friend of People of Color: White Investments in Anti-Racism." *International Journal of Qualitative Studies in Education* 16, no. 1 (2003): 7–29.

12. Ibid.

13. Helms, Janet E., "Toward a Model of White Racial Identity Development," in *Black and White Racial Identity: Theory, Research, and Practice* (Santa Barbara, CA: Green-wood Press, 1990), 49–66.

14. Cabrera, Nolan L., Jesse S. Watson, and Jeremy D. Franklin. "Racial Arrested Development: A Critical Whiteness Analysis of the Campus Ecology." *Journal of College Student Development* 57, no. 2 (2016): 119–134.

15. Ibid.

16. Lasher, Megan, "Read the Full Transcript of Jesse Williams' Powerful Speech on Race at the BET Awards," *TIME*, last modified June 27, 2016, http://time.com/4383516/jesse-williams-bet-speech-transcript/.

17. Chan, Melissa, "Justin Timberlake Sorry after Angry Response to Jesse Williams Tweet," *TIME*, last modified June 27, 2016, http://time.com/4383423/justin-timberlake-jesse-williams-speech/.

18. Kane, Kim, "Dear Tomi Lahren: Take Several Seats," *Huffington Post*, last modified July 1, 2016, http://www.huffingtonpost.com/kim-kane/dear-tomi-lahren-take-several-seats_b_10760446.html.

19. Holdren, Sara. "Theater Review: Why I Can't Accept Admissions." *Vulture*. March 13, 2018. Accessed May 17, 2019. https://www.vulture.com/2018/03/theater-review-why-i-cant-accept-admissions.html#comments.

20. Green, Jesse. "Review: Skewering White Pieties about Diversity in 'Admissions'." *The New York Times*. March 13, 2018. Accessed May 17, 2019. https://www.nytimes.com/2018/03/12/theater/admissions-joshua-harmon-review.html.

21. Holdren, 2018.

22. "Soutik Biswas's India: How Churchill 'Starved' India." *BBC*. Accessed May 17, 2019. http://www.bbc.co.uk/blogs/thereporters/soutikbiswas/2010/10/how_churchill_starved_india.html.

23. Hari, Johann. "Not His Finest Hour: The Dark Side of Winston Churchill." *The Independent*. February 14, 2019. Accessed May 17, 2019. http://www.independent.co.uk/news/uk/politics/not-his-finest-hour-the-dark-side-of-winston-churchill-2118317.html.

24. Eddo-Lodge, Reni. "Why I'm No Longer Talking to White People about Race." *The Guardian*. May 30, 2017. Accessed June 01, 2019. https://www.theguardian.com/world/2017/may/30/why-im-no-longer-talking-to-white-people-about-race.

25. National Archives and Records Administration. Accessed May 17, 2019. https://georgewbush-whitehouse.archives.gov/news/releases/2001/07/images/20010716-3.html.

· 5 ·

WHITROGGRESSIONS: CRACKER, HONKY, BECKY, AND #KAREN

Whitroggressions are seemingly race-based prejudicial comments or actions against White people, but they are ultimately mistakenly perceived to be racist because of the absence of a structural power behind the insults. A cousin of White pain, the Whitroggression is about mis-appropriating the pain of being caricatured or stereotyped in relation to race. In recent years there has been a backlash against "snowflakes" who are considered overly sensitive—particularly on college campuses. The irony of the critique against snowflakes, trigger warnings, and sensitivity is that those making the accusations often take the same degree of offense toward issues that conflict with their own values. For example, any variation in gender identity and bathroom use may be taken as an offense. Kneeling during the National Anthem as a way of protest against police violence is seen, somehow, as an offense to the American flag and, for an added layer of drama, an offense to people who have served in the military. Someone once asked us, "Can you say anything in the classroom anymore without triggering someone?" For some, any limitation on the freedom to make racially disparaging comments about those around them is now an offense against their freedoms. But when someone takes offense to those taking offense, the polemic loses coherency. Whitroggressions are a unique kind of claim to pain and demonstrate how one manifestation of White pain is expressed in the form of pejorative applications to White identity.

Now I'm the Victim

After I (Jun) led a workshop that addressed the ongoing prevalence of racial microaggressions at university campuses across the country, a colleague bemoaned to me, that he now felt like the victim of racism and *macro*aggressions as a White man. He shared how increasingly concerned he had become over what seemed to be acceptable racialized insults and bashing of White men in particular, without any consequence. "How come everyone can make fun of and pick on White men like me, and never be called racist?" he asked in frustration. "It's not fair," he concluded as he shook his head. This gentleman would probably have much to discuss with another one of my White male colleagues from Chapter 4, who expressed his White 22 angst about not having the ability to win when it comes to any discussions of race.

We have heard similar arguments like this from White colleagues, students, and friends over the past several years: why is it okay to bash White people, but not people of color? White men are increasingly expressing feelings of being targeted and singled out and "microaggressed" when discussing race relations. The term *microaggressions* has been around for several decades but was most recently defined by psychologist Derald Wing Sue[1] as brief and commonplace daily verbal, behavioral, or environmental indignities, whether intentional or unintentional, that communicate hostile, derogatory, or negative racial slights and insults toward people of color. I (Jun) have written about my own experiences with microaggressions within the evangelical Christian community.[2] According to Sue's definition, the term racial microaggression specifically refers to slights against ethnic minorities targeted by the dominant group.

This chapter further explores microaggressions, the history of racial epithets toward White people and the construction of Whitroggressions as another strategy of defending White dominance. In Chapter 6, White wrath, we address some of the consequences and byproducts that have emerged out of this frustration of being Whitroggressed by people of color. The ultimate aim of this chapter is to explore the development of Whitroggressions and the ways in which their history reveal a deeply embedded sequence in the blueprints for the White architecture of the mind to defend White dominance.

People of color and White people often perceive derogatory racial slurs toward White people differently. Those in the dominant group often claim that they are experiencing reverse racism as a result of what some perceive as an angry, politically correct, Marxist, anti-White, and anti-American agenda.

Many who still fail to see color and defend White dominance through colorblind ideologies often find critiques of dominant systems to be inherently offensive, racist, and personally menacing. Some have expressed to us their fear of anarchy and the overthrow of American values and beliefs. Anti-racist dialogue is perceived as a threat to hard work and individual merit. From our perspective, dominant groups cannot receive slurs and negative attitudes the same way as people of color because of the dissonance between these attitudes and the benefits that are typically associated with a dominant status.

Racial Microggressions

In order to understand Whitroggressions, it is important to be familiar with the concept and impact of racial microaggressions. In general, the history and study of race has focused on overt racism and the infliction of derogatory terms on people of color. The defense of White dominance can be seen in something conspicuous, like the use of the n[word]. The argument from White people is that using it should be acceptable for them, since it is acceptable for use within the Black community. They then feel a sense of injustice and hypocrisy when told that it is not acceptable for use by White people.

Although overt racism still exists in many forms, the expansion in understanding *micro*forms of racism has become both prominent and valuable. The earliest explanation from 1974 used the Black and White binary to highlight that:

> [t]hese assaults to black dignity and black hope are incessant and cumulative. Any single one may be gross. In fact, the major vehicle for racism in this country is offenses done to blacks by whites in this sort of gratuitous never-ending way. These offenses are microaggressions. Almost all black-white racial interactions are characterized by white put-downs, done in automatic, pre-conscious, or unconscious fashion. These mini-disasters accumulate. It is the sum total of multiple microaggressions by whites to blacks that has pervasive effect to the stability and peace of this world.[3]

The study and impact of racial microaggressions is essential to understanding race relations. Microforms of aggression and assault create hostile environments in which to work or study. They have real impacts on mental and physical health, and they lower productivity and perpetuate inequities. Although a paper cut or bee sting may be a small injury, the effect of a mass accumulation of those small injuries over a lifetime is severe. The cumulative impact of microaggressions is like death by a thousand White paper cuts.

As the recognition of the impact of microaggressions expands, the resistance to acknowledging their impact also increases. As with other methods for defending White dominance, the ability to make similar claims in the White experience denies the significance of the race-connected explanations of how people of color experience the world. Consequently, Whitroggressions constitute a claim to being the target of slurs in order to devalue the legitimacy of the experiences of people of color. Although there is indeed a history of slurs toward White people, especially as it relates to class, it is our assertion that the influence of power and privilege mitigate the systemic impact of the verbal slights.

Outbreeding the Trash

Derogatory terms have been used to insult White people across regions in the United States. These types of terms exist across cultures around the world. Negative descriptors such as cracker, honky, redneck, hillbilly, White boy, and White trash are just a few Whitroggressions. Other terms, such as *haole*, *gringo*, Anglo, and Caucasian have been used as neutral descriptors of White people, but have also been seemingly co-opted terms that have led to feelings of Whitroggressions for some in the dominant group.

Although certain aspects of the term Whitroggression will highlight White fragility, the history of the White underclass in the U.S. highlights another aspect of the concept—fear of losing dominance, even from within the White race. In the mid-1800s, the notions of imperial destiny and biological determinism were strong, and the idea that there was a superior "American blood" became prominent. As a result, the advancement of the race had to occur through selecting sexual partners of the same blood.[4] The frenzy became more "scientific" and evolved into eugenics, the social philosophy constructed around improving human genetics through increasing sexual reproduction for desired traits and decreasing or sterilizing reproduction of undesirable traits.

The Racial Integrity Act of 1924 proscribed interracial marriages. This law defined White as having no trace of any blood but Caucasian and was followed by the 1927 landmark decision in *Buck v. Bell* giving the government the ability to regulate breeding among citizens. Chief Justice Oliver Wendell Holmes found sterilization to be a civic duty in order to filter out incompetence. Accordingly, the 1920s saw "social exclusiveness masquerade as science and disdain for rural backwardness."[5]

Nancy Isenberg, author of the book *White Trash*, argued that the use of derogatory terms for lower class Whites is a central narrative that proves an obsession in American society over labels we give to people we do not wish to notice. The history of the White underclass can be taken multiple ways. One perspective highlights the ways in which class plays a serious role in domination and oppression (as it does with regard to the primary topic of this project—race). As the White underclass was segregated into a separate race and sterilized out of fear of inbreeding, there are clear examples of the intersections and creations of class and race oppression.

In the same era as the Racial Integrity Act, the Immigration Restriction Act of 1924 set limits on the entry of southern and eastern European immigrants, and the Deportation Act of 1929 allowed for the removal of Mexicans who crossed the border. Italian and Irish immigrants were not considered White upon their arrival to the U.S., but David Roediger demonstrated how they were able to achieve Whiteness.[6] This "achievement" largely occurred through consorting with the dominant White race to make sure that people of color remained on the bottom of the hierarchy. The White underclass eventually benefited from this arrangement and found greater opportunities for social mobility. Eugenics, the history of White trash, and the legal construction of what it means to be White ultimately worked together to maintain a racial hierarchy.

The history of the construction of Whiteness began well before the twentieth century. For example, before the Racial Integrity Act, the U.S. created immigration policies that required proving Whiteness for citizenship. These early immigration policies and then later exclusion acts that specifically excluded certain non-White races, such as the Chinese Exclusion Act, served as the foundation for constructing Whiteness as a U.S. standard for inclusion, citizenship, and social power. Because history repeats itself, new government actions appear with similar disdain toward perceived outsiders. As a contemporary example, in January 2017, President Trump signed an Executive Order banning people from seven predominantly Muslim countries from entering the U.S. The order also suspended entry to the U.S. for all Syrian refugees.

Understanding this history is key to understanding Whitroggressions. Although Whitroggressions may be interpreted as a slur and often feel painful, the history of Whitroggressions reveals a deeply embedded sequence in the blueprints for the White architecture of the mind, which is called upon knowingly or unknowingly to defend White dominance. In order to understand how Whitroggressions function, let us consider several popular terms and their historical roots.

"Cracker" as a racial epithet has been in use for several hundred years. Comedian Chris Rock's album, *Bigger and Blacker*, includes a sketch where he is depicting the dual nature of how a Black person may approach talking with someone who is White. Initially the tone is along the lines of, "How you doing, sir? Pleased to meet you. Whatever I can get you, you let me know." Then, Rock goes on to say,

> As soon as the White man get out of sight, he's like: 'Cracker-ass cracker! I'll put my foot in the crack of your ass, cracker-ass cracker! I wish that cracker would've said some shit to me, saltine-assed, motherfucking cracker!'[7]

Cracker evolved into a White racial slur beginning as early as the 1700s, and has been synonymous with impostors, trespassers, and unpoliced squatters who took resources like crops, timber, animals, and fish from land they did not own. The term first appeared in British official records in the 1700s to describe lawless noisy braggers who were prone to lying, vulgarity, and who could "crack" a crude joke.[8] The lineage of the term evolved and also became applicable to poor White people who managed slaves but did not own land. Leading up to the Civil War, the terms squatter and cracker (as well as the indignation about poor White people acting like Native Americans/Indians) had faded from common use.

The expression "poor White trash" evolved as an enduring insult for the diseased and degenerate spawn of White folks.[9] In some ways, White trash southerners became a subset of their own race, with a much lower status. Some have argued that the word emerged from the days of chattel slavery in the United States, for poor White field workers who cracked their whips. In 2006 Dana Ste. Claire wrote about the history of crackers in Florida and found that the derogatory term referred to Celtic (Scotch Irish) immigrants who settled in the southeast part of the United States.[10] They were viewed as an unruly group with poor manners who lived off the land as homesteaders, and thus were looked down upon by broader society.

"Honky" is another White racial slur that is arguably a derivative term for Hunky, a derogatory term for Hungarian immigrants in the early 1900s who were mostly poor, low-wage laborers, and thus looked down upon in society. As White Europeans continued to arrive on U.S. shores, derogatory terms for different nationalities were prevalent; but over time, as Roediger[11] and his colleague[12] pointed out, people of European ancestry slowly became White.

"Redneck" is a derogatory term rooted historically to insult poor White rural farmers in the south in the nineteenth century. In his book *Redneck Manifesto*,[13] author Jim Goad challenges the notion that racism can only come from people in power within a system. He argues that poor Whites are called rednecks and are made the butt of many jokes by all other ethnic groups with impunity.

Haole, a term used by native peoples of Hawai'i, was originally meant to describe any non-indigenous Hawaiian. It now primarily refers to White people living in Hawai'i. Charles Kenn[14] alleged that the term literally translated as "one without breath," in reference to the way European explorers were seen greeting one another without exchanging breaths, which was the traditional way native Hawaiians greeted one another. Though interesting, this interpretation is not widely confirmed by Native Hawaiian scholars. Although holding residence over time in Hawai'i may afford White folks a special category, the term *haole* is tied to ongoing issues of sovereignty, colonization, and belonging. However, as many activists in Hawai'i continue to fight for independence and sovereignty from the White colonization that illegally occupied the island nation, the presence of White foreigners continues to be a source of conflict and derision, and the word *haole* has been used to signify the pain. Similarly, the word *gringo*, which has Mexican roots and refers to White foreigners, has its origin in the Spanish word for Greek. The word has been used broadly to refer both positively and negatively to U.S. citizens, Europeans, and Latinx who speak little or no Spanish.

We agree that intentional verbal insults and racial slurs, including those targeting White people, are not only uncharitable but also demeaning. We also submit that a system of racism is nevertheless in place and perpetuated along the lines of a dominant group, and that even well-educated people of color for several generations in the United States have continued to experience structural discrimination based on race. While we acknowledge the inappropriateness of these terms, we also acknowledge the inappropriateness of comparing these terms to those employed against people of color. Due to the system of racism providing the structure of our society, pejorative terms against people of color continue to stabilize that very structure of inequality. When White people offer Whitroggressions as an example of racial offense, it does not take into account their benefits in the racialized system in place. Equating their offense with racial microaggressions against ethnic minorities only serves to exert their own dominance, thereby supporting the overarching structure in place. All offenses are not equal, and employing White pain through examples of Whitroggressions ends up min-imizing the larger injustices in society.

The Problem with Caucasian

Caucasian has long been used synonymously with White. Critics take excep-tion to the word as pejorative because of the term's geographic roots.[15] The term literally references the mountainous Caucasus region near the indepen-dent nations of Georgia and Russia. It is both problematic and ironic as a racial classification, however, because the native people of that region are phenotypically not considered White. As a result, it is ignorant to use this geographic term as the basis for White populations who typically would locate their ancestry in Europe. An analysis of the word Caucasian in books shows a spike in its use in the post-Civil Rights era (see Figure 5.1). The rise in the use of the word corresponds with the replacement of the term Black with African American, making Caucasian an attempt at sounding like a neutral, dispas-sionate, or technical term for White.

The term has its origins in the late eighteenth century, when some White men attempted to sound scientific by using the shapes of skulls to construct views of race and beauty. What is now considered the White racial category was named for a range of mountains, because a German scientist named Blumenbach constructed a racial classification system and used the name in 1795. This racist pseudo-science was used to support the notion that Germans were the most beautiful of all people. Cranium measurements, weak anthro-pology, the search for beauty, and a hierarchy of races led to the creation

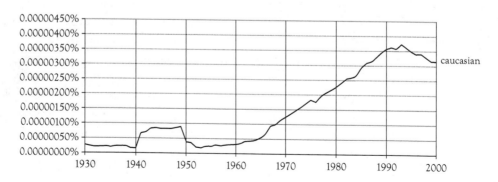

Figure 5.1: Use of the Word Caucasian in Books from 1930 to 2000

and use of the term Caucasian. According to Stephen Jay Gould, the use of Caucasian is a riddle that is answered by understanding Blumenbach's notion that the European variety of people is the most ideal, but in order to find a smaller group that has the highest degree of perfection, he identified the people around Mount Caucasus as those who possessed the most characteristics of the original idea. As a result, he named "the entire European race for their finest representatives."[16]

As demonstrated in Figure 5.1 and in a plethora of other examples, the frequent use of the word continues today. Even a Supreme Court justice used the word to describe a plaintiff in 2012.[17] In the end, the term has racist origins, inaccurate and ironic geographical/racial applications, and perpetuates a neutral view of the White race. For these reasons, we find that the word is conflicted and should not be used when talking about White people and White systems. We typically avoid prescriptions, but in this case, we advocate to *stop using the word Caucasian*, and if you hear it used as a way to sound neutral about race, ask people to look up the history of the word and consider being more critical about their choice of phrase.

The hypocrisy of the idea of a Whitroggression is clearly seen in the use of the word Caucasian. Despite its racist history and overall inaccuracy, most White people do not find the term inappropriate. Most people may not be aware.

Claims of Whitroggressions also point to racism and power. We define racism as prejudice multiplied by power that plays out in a system intended to benefit the dominant majority group that created that system. Naming supremacy in its unique and covert manifestations is part of an evolutionary advance toward ecological and systemic racial justice. A cousin of White Pain is Whitroggression because it is about feeling or mis-appropriating the pain of being caricatured or stereotyped in relation to race. Whitroggressions are a logical fallacy—individual feeling and individual pain for White people being called names that are weaponized to distract from the systemic racialized realities for a vast majority of people of color.

The N[word] for White People

Of all the negative terms, slanderous words, and offensive comments levied against White people over the centuries, we have found that there is one word that makes White people most defensive—*racist*. The r[word] has been referred to as the n[word] for White people—not because of the actual severity of the word, but rather the reaction it garners from White folks. We recognize and acknowledge that there is no White equivalent for the n[word], because no word for Whiteness can encapsulate 400 years of enslavement followed by legal maneuvering to perpetuate the poor treatment of the formerly enslaved through a series of Jim Crow laws.

Defensive postures emerge and the White architecture of the mind is exposed whenever the word racist is invoked. A common defense tactic is one of two approaches, or maybe both: A first response is a denial that one is *personally* racist. This reaction speaks perhaps to the individualistic nature of White people and culture in Western society. The second is the opposite response—the assertion that *everyone* is racist, and that therefore any accusations of specifically White people being racist are rejected out of hand.

I (Jun) had an interaction with someone who wrote this defense that encapsulates frustrations with what he would agree with are ongoing Whitroggressions:

> Everyone is racist. Not just members of the majority White race in America but everyone! I think that everyone from every culture can be racist, including minorities, especially when they exclude White people. How can there be minority only meetings and clubs like Black Student Unions, Asian only fraternities and sororities, where no Whites are allowed? The radical idea of racial justice only oppresses White people. When scholarships are granted solely by race, again White people are excluded, and money is available only to minorities, Whites are now consistently denied funds to help with their studies. This is reverse racism. When minorities look at someone from the majority culture and assume that person got there by privilege, this is prejudice and racism.[18]

This exchange illustrates that Whitroggressions provoke a feeling that manifests into the ongoing denial of systemic racism, based on one's personal lived experiences, interpreted through a dominant lens, and accompanied by cries of reverse racism that presuppose an already post-racial and post-Civil Rights leveled playing field. This individual believes in a myth of meritocracy that reassures White people that hard work, aspiration, and risk taking are the keys to success, and people of color are to blame for their failures. The logic fails to recognize the systemic nature of racialized oppression. Eradicating or reducing the possibility of being identified as a White racist further obscures the direction of the power dynamic and obfuscates historical and systemic inequities.

Becky and Shaniqua

A White person who refers to any Black woman as a "Shaniqua" is likely making a racist comment that stereotypes and essentializes Black people. The colloquial use of the word has evolved with vitriol, as represented by the description in the Urban Dictionary: "Shaniqua—A stereotypical name for young women living in the hood or ghetto."[19]

Much to the surprise of many White folks, the name "Becky" is a pejorative used for White women in some Black spaces. The year 2016 reintroduced the racialized moniker as singer Beyoncé releasing her hit music video, "Lemonade." Among the empowered, politically layered, and racially controversial themes, one provocative and highly publicized lyric is: "He better call Becky with the good hair." The Becky and Shaniqua comparison raised the question in some circles of whether it is racist for Black women to refer to White women as Becky.

Television host Wendy Williams[20] responded to the controversy by stating, "Calling a white girl 'Becky' … is like calling a black girl 'Shaniqua.'" Others were quick to defend Beyoncé, acknowledging that while Becky is generally a negative descriptive term, it was not a racist epithet. Historically the name first appeared in William Makepeace Thackeray's 1847 novel, *Vanity Fair*.[21] Thackery's protagonist, Becky Sharp, was portrayed as a social climber who used her charm to seduce men. Cara Kelly of *USA Today*[22] offered a brief history of Becky, from Thackery to Mark Twain's 1876 novel Tom Sawyer, where Becky Thatcher seduces Tom. The name Becky appears in the 1992 music video "Baby Got Back" by Sir Mix A Lot, where Becky is portrayed as a clueless White woman. The name over time has become a Black cultural reference to White women. Again, it is unclear to what extent most White women have been either aware of or offended by the reference. Anecdotally, our experience with our White colleagues has been mixed, with perhaps much being dependent upon the degrees of exposure White women have to Black communities and Black creative expression.

The Birth of #BBQBecky and Friends

While it may be tempting to think that Whitroggressions only refer to older, obvious, and well-known terms, we must consider the fluidity and movement of language that has given us new names and concepts. In what follows we recognize a variety of new names, monikers, racial epithets and a series of hashtags (#BBQBecky, #PermitPatty, #PoolPatrolPaula, #CouponCarl, and #Karen) that are used to shame racist White behaviors and that have been perpetuated with a fair amount of glee on social media.

Dr. Jennifer Shulte is a Bay Area woman who now bears a new moniker, "BBQ Becky." "BBQ" was added to "Becky" (which, again, has become synonymous with self-righteous White women monitoring the behavior of people of color) when Dr. Shulte infamously called the police on two Black men who were apparently barbecuing with a charcoal grill in a non-designated area. She first reported a call to the police on Sunday morning of April 29, 2018, because she believed that it was illegal to have a charcoal grill in the park at Lake Merritt, located in the city of Oakland, California. Police recordings of the exchanges reveal that she clearly identified the people she reported as African Americans. Police transcripts have more recordings of BBQ Becky calling back after two hours, much more hysterical, claiming that she was being harassed.

The police dispatcher on the second, extended conversation can be heard asking BBQ Becky if she lives at the park and if she has a history of mental illness. When asked by the police dispatcher if she was White, Becky exclaimed that her race did not matter. Cell phone footage as well as the dispatch recordings were made public and captured the majority of the exchange with a concerned citizen who publicly questioned her for the duration of time that it took Oakland PD to arrive at the scene of the public park. Toward the end of the video footage, BBQ Becky is visibly upset, shaking, crying, and claiming that she has been harassed—somehow, she became the victim. The two friends who were originally barbecuing that fateful Sunday morning, Kenzie Smith and his friend Onsayo "Deacon" Abram, have stated in an interview that she referred to them as n[word] and threatened that they would be going to jail for barbecuing with charcoal.[23] Dr. Shulte's paranoia about two Black men cooking in the park, her intentionality in calling the police, and her proclaimed victimhood in light of their presence earned her the hashtag BBQBecky.

#PermitPatty

In the neighboring city of San Francisco in June 2018, shortly after the incident in Oakland, "Permit Patty," whose real name is Alison Ettel, was caught on camera confronting an eight-year-old Black girl who was selling water at AT&T Park. Permit Patty can be seen on video footage, recorded by the girl's mother, calling the police. In an interview with CNN, Ettel, who ultimately resigned as CEO of a cannabis related business, TreatWell Health, said she initially complained about the noise, but as events escalated she called the police about a permit.[24] Though Permit Patty did not garner the same level of attention as BBQ Becky, the event helped cement the fact that naming and publicizing White people harassing people of color with claims of violating civil code can be an act of resistance.

#GolfcartGail

Since the BBQ Becky and Permit Patty incidents, other nicknames and hashtags have emerged as a result of White people calling police on people for engaging in everyday activities. "Golfcart Gail," for example, was a White woman who called the police about a Black father at a youth soccer match in October 2018 for allegedly yelling at the referees, when he was instructing his son to listen to his coach.[25] Golfcart Gail, who served as a field marshal at the community park in Florida, is seen on video footage following the Black father around in her golf cart. She called the police when he attempted to leave, stating that she no longer felt safe.

#PoolPatrolPaula

At a community pool in Summerville, North Carolina in June 2018, Stephanie Sebby-Strempel, a White woman who has been nicknamed "Pool Patrol Paula," was charged with assaulting a Black teenaged male. She approached a Black boy at a public pool and told him he did not belong there. She called him n[word] and chased him out of the pool and struck him with her hand. A police report concluded that Sebby-Strempel was clearly the aggressor in this unprovoked assault. Pool Patrol Paula was charged with one count of assault and battery for the incident at the community pool.[26]

#CouponCarl

Coupon Carl is a White man who worked at a CVS drug store in Chicago in July 2018. Coupon Carl emerged as a slur for White men because he had accused CVS customer, Camilla Hudson, of using a fake coupon for a $17.99 personal medical item purchase she attempted to make with a coupon mailed to her by the product manufacturer. The video footage, captured by Hudson, shows Coupon Carl, whose real name is Morry Matson, calling police and providing a description of Hudson.[27] CVS Health fired Mr. Matson along with another manager for their actions and issued an apology to Ms. Hudson. Perhaps what is most striking for us (as we watched the video footage more times than we care to confess) is that Coupon Carl can be seen visibly shaking throughout the phone conversation with the police. The video of the man demonstrates the amount of fear that may exist for some White people when interacting with Black people.

#Karen and Beyond

The emerging White viral caricatures of BBQ Becky, Permit Patty, Pool Patrol Paula, Coupon Carl, and many others represent a naming of White people who have felt their White spaces threatened. The invasion of everyday activities for White people, that have been normative in the absence of the presence of people of color, were transformed into perceived threats. Despite their humorous poignancy, these names and hashtags created by viral videos will not systemically disenfranchise White people or people named Becky. At best, the unwanted attention may help to keep White people from systemically disenfranchising people of color because of their sense of ownership, space, and fear of invasion. The nicknames are a way of recognizing the White reactions to feelings of loss as a result of daily integration in both public and private spaces.

#Karen is slang term and a meme for a cultural amalgamation of a stereotypical woman who is assertive, and in the more caricature version, an entitled, obnoxious, and middle-aged White woman. #Karen features typically include having a blonde bob haircut, always wanting to speak to a manager to lodge a complaint, driving an SUV (with kids on the way to soccer practice), making many trips to Hobby Lobby to get a new "Live, Laugh, Love" sign for the front door, going to church and book clubs that serve White wine with ice cubes, and dropping boxes of raisins into Halloween buckets. Anyone caricatured as an irritating White woman may be referred to as a Karen.

In the end these stories and hashtags are generated from White people who have been overly diligent in their belief in a duty to monitor society. Their belief in this commitment often leads to calling the police over nothing more than their own fear of Black people.[28] The hashtag #ExistingWhileBlack highlights the unimaginable ways that Black people have been stopped and questioned as a result of a White call to monitor "suspicious behavior." Most of the complainers became Instagram-infamous and promptly shamed in social media, and what remains are nicknames, hashtags, and memorable memes in social media perpetuity.

Derogatory terms about White people have been around for generations, and have been used to insult and highlight differences. Many White people have invariably taken offense to these pejorative words at different times, and we would acknowledge that while some are playful, others are painful. The shaming tags in recent years are creative cultural expressions that arise out of exasperation with White ignorance and overt racism, while others are long-standing pejoratives of a slightly different caliber. Using any epithet against another is unkind and should be avoided in reference to individuals. Our intent in this chapter is not to convey any additional moral judgment toward individuals who have uttered these words. The challenge of a Whitroggression is manifold. Any verbal insult that is conscious and intentional along the lines of race ought to be checked and corrected. However, the notion of an already leveled playing field remains problematic.

In an effort to further distinguish individual slights from systemic racial injustice, and microaggressions as distinct from Whitroggressions, please consider the following:

- Recognize the difference between a racial slur against a person of color and a racial slur against a White person. A racial slur against a person of color is a reach back into hundreds of years of systemized terrorism and racism against non-White members of American society. These racial slurs come with a history, and with that history comes power centered in a dominant group. Whether the speaker knows it or not, this historical oppressive power carries with it the perpetuation of White dominance.
- A racial slur that appears to be against a White *individual* can be a slight against this oppressive *system* itself. Criticizing White people is criticism of the White system that has oppressed people of color. Whitroggressions are a way of questioning and criticizing—or sometimes laughing at—the ways of being and acting that have created the dominantly White culture in which we find ourselves today.
- A microaggression against a person of color says, "Whether I know it or not, I am demonstrating power over you." Conversely, a slight against racist White activities communicates, "I am challenging this White dominant system of power."

A key distinction is rooted in the gap between systemic racial injustices related to the dynamics of power against people of color versus individualized expressions of racial prejudice for people of color against Whiteness.

Evolving Forward to Justice

Whitroggressions are about recognizing power perpetuated through a system. The lack of power for people of color is a critical element in the equation that makes Whitroggressions such a powerful tool of supremacy and mis-appropriation. Our concept of Whitroggressions acknowledges the verbal insult against White people while simultaneously challenging Whiteness. White people who feel that they are now victims of racism and thus feel there is equality in the levels of racism fail to grasp the systemic nature of power and dominance.

Because naming is part of our strategy, we also suggest how to use the name. When one sees examples of White caricatures producing mis-appropriated racial pain, ask yourself, *Do I feel Whitroggressed—stereotyped for my Whiteness?* If so, following the acknowledgment of the feeling, engage with the question of how the caricature impacts systemic power. The ultimate answer is that viral caricatures can help fight against the systemic power of Whiteness despite it being felt like an individual aggression toward a White person. It needs to be disentangled in order to evolve beyond the individual feeling and into the realm of interdependence and community.

A final Whitroggression is the use of the word wypipo—the phonetic spelling of "White people" in African American Vernacular English often used as social media slang to call out behaviors of White people. Journalist Michael Harriot argues that not all White people are wypipo, and that the two should not be confused or used interchangeably.

In a 2017 article Harriot wrote that:

All white people–to varying degrees–benefit from white privilege, and most white people refuse to acknowledge it–but wypipo get angry that the phrase even exists. Wypipo live under the comfortable delusion that we all live on an equal playing field. They believe the egocentric idea that success comes from hard work and ability alone, and that race doesn't play any part in their success. White people use the aphorism that some people "were born on third base, and think they hit a triple," but wypipo believe that anyone who doesn't reach base must not be as good a hitter, or doesn't practice hard enough.

The use of wypipo by *The Root*, as a section of their website, highlights the utility of Whitroggressions as a strategy of resistance to supremacy. Name-calling is not okay, but to evolve in a collective critical racial conciousness, recognizing and even joining the resistance is an imperative that outweighs embracing and/or feigning offense.

Notes

1. Sue, Derald Wing. Microaggressions in Everyday Life: Race, Gender, and Sexual Orientation. Hoboken, NJ: John Wiley & Sons, 2010.
2. Jun, Alexander. "Unintentional Racism," in *Heal Us, Emmanuel: A Call for Racial Reconciliation, Representation, and Unity in the Church*, ed. Doug Serven (Oklahoma City: Black White Bird Press, 2016), 21–26.
3. Pierce, Chester. "Psychiatric Problems of the Black Minority." *American Handbook of Psychiatry* 2 (1974): 512–523.
4. Isenberg, Nancy. *White Trash: The 400-Year Untold History of Class in America*. New York: Penguin, 2016.
5. Ibid. 205.
6. Roediger, David R. *Working toward Whiteness: How America's Immigrants became White: The Strange Journey from Ellis Island to the Suburbs*. New York: Basic Books, 2006.
7. Rock, Chris. Bigger and Blacker (DVD). HBO Studios (1999).
8. Isenberg, Nancy. *White Trash: The 400-Year Untold History of Class in America*. New York: Penguin, 2016.
9. Ibid.
10. Claire, Dana Ste. *Cracker: The Cracker Culture in Florida History*. Gainesville, FL: University Press of Florida, 2006.
11. Roediger, Working toward whiteness.
12. Barrett, James R., and David Roediger. "How White People Became White." in *White Privilege: Essential Readings on the Other Side of Racism*, ed. Paula S. Rothenberg. New York: Worth Publishers, (2002): 29–34.
13. Goad, Jim. *The Redneck Manifesto: How Hillbillies Hicks and White Trash Became America's Scapegoats*. New York: Simon and Schuster, 1998.
14. Kenn, Charles W. "What is a Haole?" Paradise of the Pacific (August 1944): 16.
15. Khan, Razib. "Stop Using the Word 'Caucasian' to Mean White," *Discover Magazine*, last revised January 22, 2011, http://blogs.discovermagazine.com/gnxp/2011/01/ stop-using-the-word-caucasian-to-mean-white/#.V6DyOpOAOko.
16. Gould, Stephen Jay. *The Mismeasure of Man*. New York: Norton, 1996, p. 410.
17. Dewan, Shaila, "Has 'Caucasian' Lost Its Meaning?" *The New York Times*, last revised July 6, 2013, http://www.nytimes.com/2013/07/07/sunday-review/has-caucasian-lost-its-meaning.html?_r=0.
18. This is quoted from someone's FB comment, from a group from which I removed myself. All writing errors were in the original.

19. "Shaniqua." *Urban Dictionary*. Accessed May 28, 2019. https://www.urbandictionary.com/define.php?term=shaniqua.

20. Williams, Wendy, "Rita Ora the Real 'Becky'?!" *The Wendy Williams Show*, Last modified April 26, 2016, https://www.youtube.com/watch?v=QCM22u6gFVQ.

21. Thackeray, William Makepeace. *Vanity Fair*. Oxford: Wordsworth Editions, 1992.

22. Kelly, Cara, "What Does Becky Mean? Here's the History Behind Beyoncé's 'Lemonade' Lyric that Sparked a Firestorm," *USA Today*, last revised April 27, 2016 http:// www.usa-today.com/story/life/entertainthis/2016/04/27/what-does-becky-mean-heres-history-be-hind-beyoncs-lemonade-lyric-sparked-firestorm/83555996/.

23. Chang, Momo. "Kenzie Smith Speaks Out." *East Bay Express*. April 15, 2019. Accessed April 17, 2019. https://www.eastbayexpress.com/oakland/kenzie-smith-speaks-out/Content?oid=16513492. The police assessed whether BBQ Becky would be eligible for a "5150"—this is the number of the section of the Welfare and Institutions Code in the state of California which allows a person with a mental illness to be involuntarily detained for a 72-hour psychiatric hospitalization. Two important highlights of this case are (1) that a White woman can go from predator to prey in an instant, claiming victimization and harassment for an altercation that she initiated; and (2) that the default diagnosis in the face of racism from white people is mental illness. Somehow it seems more plausible to authorities that mental illness rather than racism would be the root cause for the behaviors of mass murderers, school shooters, and domestic terrorists; this perhaps reveals much about the collective White architecture of the mind in U.S. society.

24. Smith, Emily and Eric Levenson. "After Internet Mockery, 'Permit Patty' Resigns as CEO of Cannabis-Products Company." *CNN*. June 27, 2018. Accessed April 17, 2019. https://www.cnn.com/2018/06/25/us/permit-patty-san-francisco-trnd/index.html.

25. "White Woman Dubbed 'Golfcart Gail' Calls Police on Black Father at Soccer Game." *NBCNews.com*. Accessed April 17, 2019. https://www.nbcnews.com/news/us-news/white-woman-dubbed-golfcart-gail-calls-police-black-father-soccer-n921121.

26. Zdanowicz, Christina. "A White Woman Allegedly Hit a Black Teen, Used Racial Slurs and Told Him to Leave a Pool. Then She Bit a Cop." *CNN*. June 29, 2018. Accessed April 18, 2019. https://www.cnn.com/2018/06/29/us/pool-patrol-paula-south-carolina-trnd/index.html.

27. Stevens, Matt. "CVS Fires 2 for Calling Police on Black Woman over Coupon." *The New York Times*. July 16, 2018. Accessed April 18, 2019. https://www.nytimes.com/2018/07/16/business/cvs-coupon-manager-black-woman-police.html.

28. Farzan, Antonia Noori. "BBQ Becky, Permit Patty and Cornerstore Caroline: Too 'Cutesy' for Those White Women Calling Police on Black People?" *The Washington Post*. October 19, 2018. Accessed April 17, 2019. https://www.washingtonpost.com/news/morning-mix/wp/2018/10/19/bbq-becky-permit-patty-and-cornerstore-caroline-too-cutesy-for-those-white-women-calling-cops-on-blacks/?utm_term=.c5f097431a48.

WHITE WRATH: MAKE AMERICA WHITE AGAIN

In January 2019, a White man who had been an officer in the U.S. military planned a massive terrorist attack. He accumulated numerous firearms and narcotics, and wrote extremist sentiments about establishing a White homeland. He studied White nationalist manifestos and conducted searches online including, *"what if trump illegally impeached," "best place in dc to see congress people," "civil war if trump impeached,"* and *"social democrats usa."*[1] His planned attack on the United States was foiled by investigators and law enforcement, even as a wall was being constructed on the Southern border to prevent "bad" people, drugs, and terrorists from entering the U.S.

In August 2017, Charlottesville, VA was host to a White supremacist demonstration called the "Unite the Right" rally. The hate groups represented at the rally included a variety of organizations that included neo-Confederates, neo-Nazis, the KKK, the Proud Boys, Identity Evropa, and many more. Prominent White supremacists present included Richard Spencer and former KKK grand wizard turned politician David Duke. Demonstrators carried a variety of objects, like confederate flags, Nazi flags, and semi-automatic weapons and shouted and chanted a variety of racially charged and incendiary comments. Several clashes occurred between protesters and counter-protesters, the worst of which was a White man who drove a car into a crowd of counter-protesters, killing a White woman named Heather Hyer. She was known for her passionate work against injustices like racism, and Spike Lee dedicated his Academy Award winning film *BlacKKKlansmen* to her.

What was also notable about the rally in Charlottesville was Donald Trump's commentary about it. When asked to comment on the rally, he said: "We condemn in the strongest possible terms this egregious display of hatred, bigotry and violence on many sides, on many sides." This quote was met with a lot of resistance, because White supremacist rallies typically do not garner vague responses that can be taken as a critique against the counter-protesters as well. A day later, Trump spoke again at a press conference and added: "You had some very bad people in that group, but you also had people that were very fine people, on both sides."[2] These remarks were consistent with Trump's record of racist rhetoric: on other occasions, he has disparaged basketball players, football players, reporters, immigrants, and people from other countries with language rife with racist, sexist, and ableist comments.

A variety of institutions have worked to track the rise in hate groups and hate incidents since Trump was elected. The Southern Poverty Law Center, the Anti-Defamation League, and the FBI, to name a few, have all demonstrated that even despite the variations in their methodology, there has been an increase in the prevalence of hate groups, hate crimes, and hate speech.[3] Even when these issues are not overtly focused on race, they are focused on their contempt for people that are not like them. Consider, for example, the Westboro Baptist Church (pictured in Figure 6.1) and their inflammatory rhetoric about Muslims, Jews, and LGBTQI+ persons. The function and proliferation of these groups is woven into a tapestry of our changing society that is increasingly characterized by the presence of White wrath.

On the evening of June 17, 2015, a young man entered a Bible study at the Emmanuel African Methodist Episcopal (AME) Church in Charleston, South Carolina. The man sat down, prayed, read the Bible, and then murdered nine Black Americans. Only one person was left alive, so she could tell the world what he had done and why—as the killer said, "You're taking over our country."[4] He was a 21-year-old White high school dropout who used violence to recapture something that he felt he was losing. Although he did not have a formal education, he was actively learning from a variety of websites, including the Council of Conservative Citizens, which has roots in the 1950s White Citizens' Council that terrorized Black people, schools, and churches.[5] He wore a jacket with the colonial flag of White-ruled Rhodesia, which existed next to apartheid-era South Africa.

Figure 6.1: Photo of Westboro Baptist Church protesters taken by author

As with many killings committed by White men, a mental health explanation of his behavior was quickly deployed to dissociate his actions from the fabric of White America. His actions were associated with his being deranged and uneducated. Although he lacked a high school diploma, he had been consuming a curriculum from the fabric of an angry subset of White America. Less than a month after this massacre, the eventual Republican presidential nominee, Donald Trump, spoke to an enthusiastic and mostly White audience with the primary promise, "Don't worry, we'll take our country back."[6]

Angry White Guys

The sentiment behind "taking the country back" has a deep historical legacy, especially as it relates to law and policy. In 2008, Barack Obama had been elected to be the first Black president of the United States of America. Around the world, the event was heralded as a victory for people of color and humanity at large. In some circles, the election was seen as the first event in a post-racial era for the United States.

Conversely, there was a great deal of dismay among political conservatives about what had occurred. Voter turnout analyses showed that, for the first time in history, the Black voting rate nearly equaled that of Whites, and that the only demographic sector that opponent John McCain dominantly won was with elderly White people and evangelical Christians.[7] The demographic voting results contributed to extensive political strategizing, but Republican Senator Lindsey Graham of South Carolina summarized the core of the issue when he said, "We're not generating enough angry White guys to stay in business for the long term."[8]

The historical legacy of the perceived loss of dominant White status started long before Obama was elected as president. It did not begin with the looming racial minority majority demographic shift in the U.S.—the moment when people of color will comprise 51% of the population. As carefully outlined by Carol Anderson, White rage is not just about physical violence, but also the way it works through the courts, legislatures, bureaucracies, and educational systems. According to Anderson, the fuel for White rage is fear of Black advancement, and even historical U.S. heroes have taken part in resisting this. For example, President Abraham Lincoln once stated, "I am not, nor ever have been, in favor of bringing about in any way the social and political equality of the white and black races," a sentiment which included opposition to Black citizens voting, serving on juries, holding public office, or marrying across races.[9] Lincoln's disposition resulted in the resettling of large amounts of free Black people in Liberia and attempts to send them to colonize Panama. He also told Black leaders that the war in the U.S. would not have happened if it were not for their race.

After Barack Obama was elected in 2008, many wondered if the United States was entering a post-racial era. But at the end of his presidency in 2016, an entirely new and energized White anger emerged to overtly defend White dominance. For example, a billboard appeared on a Tennessee road that said, "MAKE AMERICA WHITE AGAIN." In an article accompanying the same image that was on the sign, candidate Rick Tyler argued for protecting White values by stopping all non-White immigration and maximizing immigration from Rhodesia (the correct name is Zimbabwe) and South Africa.[10] Rick Tyler is not a mainstream candidate, but his advocacy represents a level of overt attitudes that are making their way into the mainstream discourse. Shortly after the Republican National Convention nominated Donald Trump as their presidential candidate, David Duke, a former KKK leader, cited Trump's candidacy as an inspiration during his announcement that he would run for an open U.S. Senate seat. He stated: "We must stop the massive immigration and ethnic cleansing of people whose forefathers created America."[11]

In the state of Oregon in January 2016, some White anti-government ranchers broke into a federally owned wildlife refuge and committed to staying there until the government ended tyranny.[12] The background to this event includes a history of resisting the federal government's oversight of land in the Western United States, grazing rights, fences, and even arson. After the occupation of the refuge started, other anti-government demonstrators joined from around the country and found ways to send supplies. Law enforcement and the government were slow to respond, which lead to the critique that if these were Muslim protesters or even the Black Lives Matter movement, they would have faced greater penalties more quickly.[13] The protesters stayed for forty-one days and often spoke to the press. Previously, key organizer Cliven Bundy articulated that Black Americans might have been better off enslaved, perhaps as a way of highlighting how bad they believe the government to be. Most of the occupiers and all of the 23 men and women arrested for felony charges were White.

If the story seems odd, it is. The history of federal land management and Western ranchers is complicated and increasingly tense. We include the event here because it is another example of overt and growing White anger from people who feel like they are losing something. It is an indication of the lengths to which White folks will go to defend their dominance when they feel the need to resist. Although there were relatively few occupiers involved in this demonstration, the levels of encouragement, support, and resources they received from across the U.S. is at least an indication of a growing sentiment.

Building Walls

President Donald Trump's campaign grew rapidly in significance. The mere chanting of "Trump! Trump! Trump!" continues to be used to invoke racial degradation. The public rhetoric by Trump, his campaign, and his broad coalition of supporters has been characterized by demeaning Mexican immigrants along with campaign promises to build a wall, broad generalizations of Muslims, and promises to stop immigration, as well as myriad other pejorative comments about women and minorities. After a Black Lives Matter protester was attacked at a Trump rally, Trump indicated, "Maybe he should have been roughed up because it was absolutely disgusting what he was doing."[14]

Since that time, there has grown a renewed sense of the way White anger can play a role in the public square and on college campuses. *The New York Times* reported:

> On campuses clenched by unforgiving debates over language and inclusion, some students embrace Mr. Trump as a way of rebelling against the intricate rules surrounding privilege and microaggression, and provoking the keepers of those rules.[15]

Trump's rhetoric has given license to a privileged majority that is working diligently to co-opt minority arguments. The fact that some in the White majority do not feel privileged gives credence to the notion that, for the privileged, equity feels like oppression. Even a White nationalist in Montana argued that Trump facilitated identity politics for White people in a way that has never been done before.[16] On college campuses, the word "Trump" has been used in ways that are being called hate speech and in conjunction with chants like "Build that wall!"

The U.S. political climate is not isolated. What is happening on college campuses and with the Trump administration is connected to events around the world. The tension around immigration is a global phenomenon, and the rhetoric infused into racialized notions of immigration is fueling tension everywhere. One of the most significant global events of 2016 was Brexit—Britain's vote to exit from the European Union. Many of the primary instigators behind the campaign to leave the European Union faded from public view after the "leave" vote won, but Theresa May took over as Prime Minister when David Cameron stepped down. She noted that one of the primary messages in the "leave" vote was to reduce immigration.[17] Even Trump connected his campaign to Brexit by emphasizing that people want their country back. The vote in Britain may be an indicator of global anxiety about immigration, a renewal of xenophobia, and a growing White rage. What happened in Britain is a growing global sentiment, and it was an early indicator that Trump would ultimately win the U.S. presidency.

Moving beyond the overt and populist nature of the Trump movement, the liberal democratic side of the political range also illuminates some aspects of suppressed White anger. Hillary Clinton was the 2016 democratic presidential nominee, but she had previously run a tough campaign against Barack Obama in 2008. During that campaign, her husband Bill Clinton made some racially laced comments about Obama and was criticized accordingly. But issues of race were (at least overtly) absent from Hillary's next failed run for the presidency. Much of her 2016 campaign was built around her status as a female candidate, including the slogan, "I'm with her." Her candidacy had consistently been depicted as breaking the highest glass ceiling for women. This essentially applies White out over the fact that she is a White woman. Instead of being identified as a *White* woman, she is just a woman, which advances the White-normative notion that all women are White. The same can be said for failed 2020 presidential candidate Elizabeth Warren. An edited volume from 1982 is an early collection of essays that disrupts this normativity—it is entitled *All the Women Are White, All the Blacks Are Men, But Some of Us Are Brave: Black Women's Studies*.[18] The result of this White-normative rhetoric is that Hillary Clinton is always presented as the first *woman* (not the first *White* woman) to be the nominee of a major party. But Barack Obama will always be the first *Black* president.

However, long before Hillary Clinton or Barack Obama, there was Shirley Chisholm. Although she is not well-known today, she was the first Black woman to be a member of congress and the first woman to run for president in the democratic primary. Her campaign slogan was "Unbought and Unbossed," and she is quoted as saying, "If they don't give you a seat at the table, bring a folding chair."[19] Chisholm was radical, groundbreaking, and disconnected from the White male political establishment. Much of the fanfare around Hillary Clinton's candidacy has done little to acknowledge Chisholm's pioneering role in U.S. politics. Although Trump evoked and invoked White anger in and around his campaign, Hillary Clinton may have been powerful for White feminism but was less favorable for racial justice.[20]

On November 9, 2016, Donald Trump was announced as the winner of the U.S. Presidential election after an Electoral College victory (Hillary Clinton won the popular vote). Various analyses of the voting demographics showed that Trump dramatically won the vote of White people without a college degree, White men, and White evangelical Christians.[21] The election came as shock, after most polls strongly predicted Clinton winning. Van Jones of CNN was visibly upset on air and called the election Whitelash against a Black president.[22]

Because of Trump's numerous comments about China, people from Mexico, Muslims, people with disabilities, and the Black community, his election came as not only a surprise to many, but left many people of color feeling unsafe. What was troubling was not just that Trump was elected, but that so many people supported his Presidency, either because of his comments or in spite of them. Either way, the wave of angry White men made a concrete move to not only make America White again, but to reveal how dominantly

White it is. Shortly after the 2016 election, President Trump signed Executive Order 13769, thus successfully placing a ban on Muslims entering the United States.[23] Under President Trump, the United States federal government shut down for thirty-five days—it was the longest U.S. government shutdown in history. The shutdown stemmed from an impasse over President Trump's demand for $5.7 billion in federal funds for the U.S.–Mexico border wall. White wrath is political and powerful.

White Student Unions and Identity

Colleges and universities are essential places for understanding society. They are also targeted by special interest groups and inflammatory speakers as places to galvanize the next generation. For example, after the White supremacist Richard Spencer was vaulted into national attention for his stiff-armed salute and "Heil Trump" speech after the election, he went on a tour speaking on college campuses. Harkening back to the activist eras of the 1960s and 1970s, colleges are places of learning and indicators of social change.

A report from the Anti-Defamation League included evidence that White supremacist speech and propaganda rapidly expanded during the 2017–2018 academic year.[24] The groups responsible for the incidents are Identity Evropa, Patriot Front, and the Daily Stormer Book Clubs. In many cases, they posted flyers that include slogans like:

- Warning! Whites Bite Back—And Good Luck Putting Us Down
- 100% European Identity 0% White Guilt

In a short span of time, other posters (see Figure 6.2) would show up on many campuses that said, "IT'S OK TO BE WHITE."[25] The posters also appeared outside the United States in both Canadian and Australian universities. These provocative reactions are ongoing evidence of White wrath. Since shifting demographics demonstrate the browning of America, many White folks feel the authority, comfort, and safety that comes from being in the dominant group slipping away. White wrath has played a critical role recently in galvanizing retrenchment.

On college campuses, the resistance against growing attention to and around diversity and multiculturalism is articulated through the formation of White student unions. At the University of California Santa Barbara

Figure 6.2: Replica of Campus Poster

(UCSB), University of Texas Austin, University of Illinois, Penn State, University of Missouri, and several other universities, White student unions have been established. The philosophies and activities of these student groups have been documented on social media, with some of them garnering almost 1,000 "likes" on Facebook. Each of these groups follow the activity of other unions and share information about the perceived indoctrination of college students with liberal perceptions of race. When the UCSB White Student Union first emerged, it was largely deemed a mockery of the Black Lives Matter movement. The origin of the union included a list of demands that mimicked the demands of BLM protesters on campuses around the country. Since then, the group has continued and appears to have an active membership with events, activities, and discussions on Facebook. The group includes a description on their Facebook home page:

> The White Student Union of University of California, Santa Barbara exists to create a safe, supportive and inclusive student community of European descent. By providing opportunities for all students to increase awareness of European culture with an emphasis on European social, political, and intellectual traditions.[26]

A traditional White response to multicultural clubs has been, "Why don't we have a White Student Union?"—echoing a similar response asking about a White History Month. Instead of acknowledging the vast majority of environments that cater to White people, White students mock ethnic minority clubs and create spaces to foster White supremacy. Using Whitroggressions as the basis for their clubs, White students display a sense of White wrath at the perceived threat against their identity. The proliferation of White student unions is yet another indicator of the growing force behind White wrath and the recapturing of something perceived as lost.

White Christian Wrath

Anger and frustration are emotions that are demonstrated in the sacred realms as well as the secular. I (Jun) have seen some of this anger emerge from White men and women in evangelical Christian communities as well. For example, in the wake of a resolution on racial reconciliation and repentance for past and present racism within the denomination, adopted in 2016 by the theologically conservative Presbyterian Church in America (PCA), an anonymous White supremacist hate group has emerged. Calling for the end of interracial marriage, separation of races in churches, and fearing the demise of churches into liberal apostasy, this angry White separatist group, representing themselves as Christians, seeks to dismantle the slow but steady work of racial justice within evangelical circles.

Having spoken at and conducted workshops for different Christian colleges and organizations as well as for nonsectarian institutions, we have seen little difference in the responses from White people. Members of both secular and sacred institutions have reacted similarly, and often with resistance and anger, when presented with ideas about systemic racism, White privilege, and a need for racial justice. It troubles us that White evangelicals seem to equate Whiteness with Christianity, and thereby unconsciously elevating their racial identity over their faith commitment.

The person of Jesus of Nazareth was a dark-skinned Jewish carpenter from the Middle East. He never spoke English and never physically lived in the United States. Most of the apostles and early church founders were from Israel-Palestine. We explored the role of Whiteness, fragility, and resistance in the book *White Jesus*. Much of the White wrath that has been manifested lately is still laced with Christian justifications and underpinnings.

The Religious White

The ideology of White evangelical Christians in America became embedded in the U.S. through the spiritualization and mass acceptance of a politicized agenda of once sacred and separated tenets of the faith. The merger of faith and politics led to the formation of a dominant system of religious White power. While many of these politicized ideas were not biblically based, religious tradition and text were manipulated to justify their widespread adoption within the White evangelical community across the United States.

White evangelical Christianity in America was exclusive and oppressive from its inception. The legacy of bad theology and the politicization of faith can be seen in the fabric of White evangelicalism today. White American Christianity might be characterized by an inability to distinguish politics from faith. Power and dominance that have been misinterpreted as God's desire become an abusive weaponization and mis-appropriation of God made in the image of dominant peoples, movements, and powers. The Son of God has been reconstructed to become White. A unique American syncretism that sought empire has led to a byproduct of American Civil religion which has conflated Christian values with American values and White values.

The image and imprint of White Jesus is a manifestation of White evangelical Christianity in America. Historians have documented how some White Christians committed horrible racial atrocities in the name of God, while a vast majority of others were complicit, audible in their silence in the face of White supremacy, allowing racism to persist with impunity. An overwhelming majority of Black Christians, along with an unpopular minority of White Christians in America, partnered in the fight against racial injustices in the 1950s and 1960s. Most were labeled "theological liberals" by orthodox leaders—a handle which could be interpreted as code for being misaligned with the true meaning of Scripture, and thus considered unbiblical and ultimately unchristian.

Christian institutions and faith-based political organizations have had a long and complex history of racial oppression. Christianity in the United States has embraced power and aligned with a conservative political ideology. The pro-life position, for example, is usually associated with a concurrent evangelical silence regarding children living in poverty, the deaths of Black citizens, mass incarcerations, the school-to-prison pipelines, and the death penalty—all of which may correctly be interpreted as pro-life positions, but which have been incredibly truncated, limiting the term "pro-life" to apply merely to pre-born fetuses in a mother's womb. Christians celebrate the bold statements of White Christian athletes such as Tim Tebow for publicly kneeling and taking up the cause of Christ, while at the same time vilifying Black Christian athlete Colin Kaepernick for publicly kneeling and taking up the cause of justice.[27] Something about Tebow's kneeling inspires White Christians, and something about Kaepernick's kneeling enrages them.

In Trevor Noah's tour, *Loud & Clear*, he acutely highlights how the "rules" are not clear in the United States. He points out that when Kaepernick put a knee on the ground during a patriotic song, he is criticized for "disrespecting the flag." The physical position is one of reverence, he is being contemplative, and certainly peaceful. But the offense claimed toward the flag and even further, members of the military, were extensive. For Noah, the rules become unclear when on the patriotic holiday, July 4th, people take to Instagram and other social media outlets to display pictures of the flag in the form of a thong or bikini where the flag is literally disappearing into their ass. This, however, is acceptable patriotism in a system where the rules are not clear.

An article published in *The Atlantic*[28] in the summer of 2016 was prophetic in its depiction of White pain and the formation of the White wrath of evangelical White Christians in America. The article cited a report published by the Public Religion Research Institute and Brookings, finding that nearly half of Americans surveyed stated that discrimination against Christians is as serious a problem as discrimination against other groups, including Blacks and minorities. The report also revealed that three-fourths of that group were Republicans and Trump supporters, and eight out of ten identified as White evangelical Protestants. In addition, the study revealed that 46% of respondents feared that immigration from Mexico and Central America has been too high in recent years.

When the same question was posed regarding immigration from predominantly Christian nations, though, only 10% of respondents stated that immigration had been too high, the article reported. The irony of course, is that this is essentially the same question, phrased two different ways: Latin American countries are overwhelmingly Christian but not White. *Atlantic* author Emma Green's analysis was at once compelling and short-sighted: she wrote that "when Americans think of those immigrants as Christians, rather than foreign nationals, they're more likely to open their arms in welcome."[29] What is missing, in both the PRRI/Brookings report as well as the article that covered it, is the unnamed and unseen Whiteness that is presumed when referring to both Americans and Christians—this is yet another form of White wrath and epistemic violence.

White Fear

On July 20, 2016, police in North Miami received a call that someone had a gun.[30] Armed and ready, officers approached Charles Kinsey, a behavioral therapist who was sitting on the ground assisting an autistic patient with a toy truck. Lying on his back on the ground, with his hands raised in the air,

Kinsey was caught on video explaining clearly and loudly that he was a behavioral therapist and that his patient only had a toy truck. A police officer shot Kinsey, an unarmed Black man, in his leg and arrested him. Although it was not captured on video, Kinsey told reporters that he asked the officer why he shot him, and the officer replied, "I don't know." It is an incredibly unfortunate scenario to shoot an unarmed Black man in July of 2016, as it falls in line with a litany of high-profile shootings by police. However, I (Collins) know why the officer shot Kinsey. I know, because the same White logic system that helped form the architecture of his mind also shaped mine.

Basic anxiety is a psychological term for the fight or flight instinct that causes people to react in a certain way when in the presence of danger. Neurotic anxiety is driven by a disordered fear and actually blocks normal anxiety and self-awareness. The construction of fear outside of basic anxiety and the accumulation of anxious feelings around a particular issue may have a herding effect. In behavioral economics, *herding* is the attraction to something when there is a group of people surrounding it (e.g., a popular place to eat, a street performer, or the new version of a smart phone). *Self-herding* is the idea that the number of times you think about buying a new item is working toward a herd of decisions that construct desire around that item.[31] By the time you make the decision to purchase it, you mentally see a herd around the item, representing you and your thoughts about making the purchase—thereby self-herding.

Seeing Black bodies as a threat creates a neurotic level of anxiety and fear. The more times this happens the greater the fear becomes. What is in fact anti-Blackness manifests in White bodies as an instinct to protect against a threat. When mental self-herding for protection against Black bodies is combined with lethal force, innocent Black behavioral therapists are shot while helping someone in need.

An Ecological View of Wrath

Sometimes efforts at protection lead to the very demise of a family, an institution, or society. The roughly translated quote from the fifth century work *The Path to Purification* discusses the effect of holding on to anger (perhaps like a weapon): "By doing this you are like a man who wants to hit another and picks up a burning ember or excrement in his hand and so first burns himself or makes himself stink."[32] Racial resentment, anger, and wrath have produced a litany of violent actions and adverse effects on the whole of society; but what is not often fully understood is the negative influence of this anger on the oppressor. In the opening chapter, in discussing epigenetics and the role of trauma, we inquired about the role effect on the inflictor of the trauma.

In a 2019 book called *Dying of Whiteness*, a physician examines the ways in which racial resentment is killing the very communities harboring the anger.[33] The examples given throughout the book focus on various policies that are supported by lower-middle class White communities that in turn produce higher death rates and shorter life spans. For example, in places where Medicaid expansion was rejected as part of an overall attack on the Affordable Care Act, White mortality has suffered. In states where guns were easily accessible, there has been a correlating increase in suicides, particularly in White communities. The author, Jonathan Metzl, leverages a respectable amount of data to support the thesis that resentment toward communities of color (and the assumption that they are pariahs subsisting on government resources) led poor White voters to vote against policies that would have improved their own health, quality of life, access to resources, and community infrastructure, including education and roads. This is spitting in the wind. The powerful role of race-baiting has worked well in galvanizing low SES White voters to inflict harm on their own ability to grow and thrive. The author returned to the age-old question of why White people resist aligning with people of color in the same income bracket. W. E. B. Du Bois demonstrated after Reconstruction that the incentive for avoiding class alignment in favor of racial alignment was the reward of being not-Black. This explains the colluding benefit for immigrants and poor Whites in accepting the benefits of White status in exchange for maintaining anti-Black racial hierarchies.

Historians have done important work to reveal the role of women in White wrath. Going back to the plantation, the book *They Were Her Property* by Stephanie Jones-Rodgers shows that White women were deeply complicit and calculating participants in the slave economy.[34] Like all systemic oppressive behaviors, there are learned habits that are passed down through the family unit. Frantz Fanon explains that society is the sum of families, and that "the white family is a guardian of a certain structure"[35]—that is, educating and training the next generation for entry into society.

So, owning slaves was also a learned behavior, and young White girls in slaveholding families were consciously prepared for this responsibility. Even as young girls, they were given enslaved Africans as gifts; they participated in managing enslaved Africans; and they participated in applying punishments to those who acted out of line. Imagine the developmental impact on children being taught to own human property, to witness brutal violence on people, and to be treated like some form of royalty. Jones-Rodgers adds, "It is important to note that young white southerners, by virtue of their skin color, were empowered by law and custom to exercise control over any enslaved person they crossed paths with"; and "[W]hen parents gave their daughters enslaved people, those daughters assumed a new identity: they became slave owners."[36]

Moving forward in history, Elizabeth McRae in *Mothers of Massive Resistance* shows that White women have been at the center of the maintenance of White supremacist politics.[37] In examining segregation and Jim Crow, she found that a variety of insidious tactics via education, withholding legal documents, racial classifications, school choice, and political action were key in preserving the power of White supremacy. By using informal networks in neighborhoods and PTA meetings, White women were able to focus on maintaining segregation in a subtle but tenacious way; and then, "They participated in the first massive support for racial segregation and later, when it was threatened, massive resistance. White women were and remained segregation's constant gardeners."[38] When combined with the role of White women on the plantation and the protections of White women as carriers of a pure race, Fanon's comments about the White family as a guardian of a certain structure begin to take shape.

As demonstrated in this chapter and elsewhere in the book, we see universities as a contested space where ideas about racial justice and equity get debated. Before students attend a university, they attend high schools that are becoming increasingly segregated, and they are living in families where behaviors are learned and passed down. Margaret Hagerman, author of the book *White Kids*, demonstrates that what parents say to their children about race has much less influence than their actions and behaviors related to race.[39] The danger here is that White wrath is now manifested through a variety of new insidious paths that may even be unknown to the family. Parents may promote narrow and uncritical perspectives like colorblindness, or they may adopt a more progressive approach, like anti-racism; but if they continue to pathologize families and neighborhoods using old racist tropes and stereotypes, it is their behavior that gets passed on to the children. Then the attitudes become a virus, and educational institutions become breeding grounds for collections of young people manifesting old and violent ideas in new ways.

Evolving against White Wrath

A socially constructed fear about people of color becomes a fixture in White systemic thinking and fuels the White architecture of the mind. A normal setting in which there is no threat (therefore no basic anxiety) becomes altered when neurotic anxiety takes over. As self-awareness decreases, repeated and fear-driven neurotic anxiety becomes self-herded in a direction; a sub- or unconscious decision is guided by neurotic anxiety. The cumulative weight of fear produces an irrational response. The phenomenon of White wrath is not limited to overtures about race and exclusion. The combination of feelings of loss and neurotic anxiety exists in a volatile space in the White architecture of the mind. It is not only about individual feelings and actions, but also about the accumulation of feelings among angry White folks dispersed across a country and even the world in a way that supports White dominance. These feelings can occur even when an individual does not know what drove their behavior or understand their actions.

When we consider the disturbing actions, events, and commentary presented in this chapter, we feel drawn to one of two approaches. The first is to isolate negative and neurotic behavior and deal with it as a personal or individual problem. The attraction of this approach is that we are alleviated from responsibility to address a person's outwardly racist behavior.

A second approach implies a more collective responsibility. In this approach, we see a tragedy like the massacre at the AME church in South Carolina as a symptom of a larger societal ill that inhabits all of our minds and bodies. Since this method is by nature more communal, we can resist the temptation to assign that action to one person, so that we can scrutinize the larger systemic feelings of loss and anxiety which are producing White wrath and maintaining forms of dominance. In order to evolve in our thinking, we must embrace a holistic approach that holds individuals accountable while also interrogating the corporate systems structuring our society and influencing our thinking.

It is not so much that angry White folks are a particular demographic as it is the observation that White wrath is a spreading sentiment around the world that recaptures a sense of what has been lost—namely, dominant Whiteness. Extensive political, educational, and violent means will be used to preserve entitlements. By revealing the phenomenon more clearly, we intend to use education to demonstrate the ways in which the sentiment is constructed, acknowledge the roles we play in preserving it, and ultimately engage in deconstruction and decolonization.

Notes

1. Bui, Lynh. "'I Am Dreaming of a Way to Kill Almost Every Last Person on Earth': A Self-Proclaimed White Nationalist Planned a Mass Terrorist Attack, the Government Says." *The Washington Post.* February 20, 2019. Accessed April 18, 2019. https://www.washingtonpost.com/local/public-safety/self-proclaimed-white-nationalist-planned-mass-terror-attack-government-says-i-am-dreaming-of-a-way-to-kill-almost-every-last-person-on-earth/2019/02/20/61daf6b8-3544-11e9-af5b-b51b7ff322e9_story.html?elq=3531d19056874e4cb45760545f6e2897&elqCampaignId=10978&elqTrackId=6d606e8b-98cf4d26bf5989361cc39582&elqaid=22298&elqat=1&noredirect=on&utm_term=.383c9a3ef367.

2. Rascoe, Ayesha. "A Year After Charlottesville, Not Much Has Changed For Trump." *NPR.* August 11, 2018. Accessed April 18, 2019. https://www.npr.org/2018/08/11/637665414/a-year-after-charlottesville-not-much-has-changed-for-trump.

3. "The Year in Hate: Rage against Change." *Southern Poverty Law Center.* Accessed April 18, 2019. https://www.splcenter.org/fighting-hate/intelligence-report/2019/year-hate-rage-against-change.

4. Dylann Roof's Racist Manifesto: "I have no choice." June 20, 2015, https://www.washingtonpost.com/national/health-science/authorities-investigate-whether-racist-manifesto-was-written-by-sc-gunman/2015/06/20/f0bd3052-1762-11e5-9ddc-e3353542100c_story.html.

5. Anderson, Carol. *White Rage: The Unspoken Truth of Racial Divide.* London: Bloomsbury Publishing, 2016.

6. Trump, Donald. "Don't Worry, We'll Take Our Country Back." July 11, 2015 http://www.nbcnews.com/politics/2016-election/donald-trump-freedomfest-you-cant-be-great-if-you-dont-n390546.

7. How Groups Voted in 2008, *Roper Center*, http://ropercenter.cornell.edu/polls/us-elections/how-groups-voted/how-groups-voted-2008/.

8. As Republican convention emphasizes diversity, racial incidents intrude. August 29, 2012, https://www.washingtonpost.com/politics/2012/08/29/b9023a52-f1ec-11e1-892d-bc92fee603a7_story.html.

9. Anderson, p. 14.

10. Make America White Again. July 18, 2016, http://ricktylerforcongress.com/2016/07/18/make-america-white-again/.

11. Former KKK leader David Duke, citing Trump, announces Senate bid. July 22, 2016, https://www.washingtonpost.com/news/powerpost/wp/2016/07/22/former-kkk-leader-david-duke-citing-trump-announces-senate-bid/#.

12. Oregon standoff: All occupiers surrender; Cliven Bundy arrested. *CNN*, February 22, 2016, http://www.cnn.com/2016/02/11/us/oregon-standoff/.

13. The Oregon Standoff, Black Lives Matter, and Criminal-Justice Reform. *The Atlantic*, January 5, 2015, http://www.theatlantic.com/national/archive/2016/01/the-oregon-standoff-debate/422556/.

14. Trump on protester: 'Maybe he should have been roughed up' November 23, 2015. *CNN*. http://www.cnn.com/2015/11/22/politics/donald-trump-black-lives-matter-protester-confrontation/.

15. For Whites Sensing Decline, Donald Trump Unleashes Words of Resistance. July 13, 2016. *The New York Times.* http://www.nytimes.com/2016/07/14/us/politics/donald-trump-white-identity.html.

16. Ibid.

17. Brexit: All you need to know about the UK leaving the EU. July 21, 2016. *BBC.* http://www.bbc.com/news/uk-politics-32810887.

18. Hull, Gloria T., Patricia B. Scott, and Barbara Smith (eds.) *All the Women Are White, All the Blacks Are Men, But Some of Us Are Brave: Black Women's Studies.* Old Westbury, NY: Feminist Press, 1982.

19. Before Clinton, Hillary. "There was Shirley Chisholm." *BBC News.* January 26, 2016. http://www.bbc.com/news/magazine-35057641.

20. Daniels, Jessie. Hillary Clinton: Good for White Feminism, Bad for Racial Justice. April 12, 2015, http://www.racismreview.com/blog/2015/04/12/hillary-clinton-good-for-white-feminism.

21. Alec Tyson and Shiva Maniam, Behind Trump's Victory: Divisions by Race, Gender, Education. *Pew Research Center,* November 9, 2016, http://www.pewresearch. org/fact-tank/2016/11/09/behind-trumps-victory-divisions-by-race-gender- education/.

22. Josiah Ryan. "'This Was a Whitelash': Van Jones' Take On the Election Results," *CNN,* November 9, 2016, http://www.cnn.com/2016/11/09/politics/van-jones-results-disappointment-cnntv/.

23. "Timeline of the Muslim Ban." *ACLU of Washington.* November 26, 2018. Accessed April 18, 2019. https://www.aclu-wa.org/pages/timeline-muslim-ban.

24. "White Supremacist Propaganda Nearly Doubles on Campus in 2017–18 Academic Year." *Anti-Defamation League.* Accessed April 18, 2019. https://www.adl.org/resources/reports/white-supremacist-propaganda-nearly-doubles-on-campus-in-2017-18-academic-year.

25. "Campuses Confront Spread of 'It's OK to Be White' Posters." Campuses Confront Spread of 'It's OK to Be White' Posters. Accessed April 18, 2019. https://www.insidehighered.com/news/2018/11/05/campuses-confront-spread-its-ok-be-white-posters?utm_source=Inside Higher Ed&utm_campaign=aaee823a62-.DNU20181105+A%2FB+Test&utm_medium=email&utm_term=0_1fcbc04421-aaee823a62-198502909.

26. UCSB White Student Union. https://www.facebook.com/UCSB-White-Student-Union-685020354966554/.

27. Frost, Michael. "Colin Kaepernick vs. Tim Tebow: A Tale of Two Christians on Their Knees." *The Washington Post.* September 24, 2017. Accessed April 18, 2019. https://www.washingtonpost.com/news/acts-of-faith/wp/2017/09/24/colin-kaepernick-vs-tim-tebow-a-tale-of-two-christianities-on-its-knees/?utm_term=.dc69af212dad&noredirect=on.

28. Green, Emma. "Most American Christians Believe They're Being Persecuted." *The Atlantic.* June 30, 2016. Accessed April 18, 2019. https://www.theatlantic. com/politics/archive/2016/06/the-christians-who-believe-theyre-being-persecuted-in-america/488468/?utm_campaign=the-atlantic&utm_content=5cb82b300f1c-fa0001e6afae_ta&utm_medium=social&utm_source=facebook.

29. Ibid.

30. Chokshi, N. (July 21 2016). North Miami Police Officers Shoot Man Aiding Patient With Autism. *The New York Times.* Retrieved from: http://www.nytimes.com/ 2016/07/22/us/north-miami-police-officers-shoot-man-aiding-patient-with-autism.html?_r=0.

31. Ariely, Dan. *Predictably Irrational: The Hidden Forces that Shape Our Decisions*. New York: Harper Collins, 2008.

32. Buddhaghosa, and Ñāṇamoli. *The Path of Purification = Visuddhimagga*. Kandy, Sri Lanka: Buddhist Publication Society, 2010. p. 297.

33. Metzl, Jonathan. *Dying of Whiteness: How the Politics of Racial Resentment Is Killing America's Heartland*. New York: Basic Books, 2019.

34. Jones-Rogers, Stephanie E. *They Were Her Property: White Women as Slave Owners in the American South*. New Haven: Yale University Press, 2019.

35. Fanon, p. 127.

36. Jones-Rodgers, pp. 15, 17.

37. McRae, Elizabeth Gillespie. *Mothers of Massive Resistance: White Women and the Politics of White Supremacy*. New York, NY: Oxford University Press, 2018.

38. McRae, p. 19

39. Hagerman, Margaret A. *White Kids: Growing Up With Privilege in a Racially Divided America*. New York: New York University Press, 2018.

· 7 ·

WHITE NOISE: STATIC, ECHOES, AND AMPLIFIERS

As a manifestation of the White architecture of the mind, *White noise* is the fruit that grows from a root system buried deep in White logic. The noise represents a disruption to understanding the impact and influence of racism and White supremacy on social systems. Rhetoric concerning race and mental frameworks for interpreting racial reasoning has been taught and cultivated over time. This chapter offers examples of White noise to understand the logic of racial resistance in an effort to evolve toward racial consciousness. White noise includes defensive posturing, justification, rationales, and the apologetics of a codified White logic system used in the face of ongoing racism in the United States.

White noise falls into three categories: *White static, White echoes, and White amplifiers*. White static is an attempt to scramble a signal—to interrupt an intended message by obscuring, obfuscating, and distracting. This is a manifestation of White logic that takes diversity-mindedness away from evolution toward racial justice. It focuses instead on maintaining supremacy (regardless of a speaker's intent). White echo is the way in which White logic becomes embedded outside of White bodies and systems, and within people of color. This is a delicate matter to include here, but it is essential to name it. A White amplifier is a cousin to the White echo. It not only mimics the original dominant voices, but amplifies them and carries the sound farther.

White supremacy is not only embodied in White people, but can also shape the thinking of people of color. In this way, colonization of the mind leads to White noise that emerges from people of color in the form of an echo. Whether or not the echo is produced consciously, it supports White dominance. This idea has been discussed in a variety of ways, primarily regarding skin tone—suggesting that some people of color who are White-passing or who benefit from light-skin privilege may echo White noise in order to maintain their social status. We are not addressing the issue of colorism exactly, but rather the interaction between systemic noise of White supremacy and the way it finds an echo and an amplifier even within people of color.

White Static

Some of the most effective rhetoric is repeated in an attempt to scramble efforts toward racial justice and maintaining White dominance. White static is similar to a mobile phone jammer, which deliberately transmits signals on the same radio frequencies to disrupt the communication between the sender and receiver. This effectively disables mobile phones within the range of the jammer. This section identifies some typical rhetorical forms of signal jamming.

White static is a cacophony that results from a collection of defensive reactions and verbal responses, revealing a logic system that refuses to acknowledge privilege, defends dominance, shifts blame to victims, claims victimization, obsesses over reverse racism, and perpetuates propaganda about the oppression of the dominant White majority. White static is a descriptor for all the distractions that keep a person from recognizing that there is a problem. These objections and rejections are the architectural and neurological blockades that prevent racial consciousness and evolution. Static functions in White systems by manufacturing chaos and distraction, forcing attention away from the central message about social inequities.

White people, as well as some folks of color, offer myriad excuses for denying the existence of both internalized racism and systemic racism in society. It happens almost instinctively, like an automated or involuntary response. It represents everything that becomes a defense of White dominance and White logic. Often the defense mechanisms lead to *Whitesplaining*—a term in the modern lexicon for a White explanation for the true nature of race problems. Claims to absolute White truth, are in fact big and little White lies.

One of the most common forms of White static is White tears. White tears happen when a White person is confronted with his or her racist words and actions. Nothing obfuscates the encounter of being called out on racism more than tears. Scholars and public intellectuals like Angela Davis, Kimberlé Crenshaw, Brittney Cooper, and others have advanced the most critical scholarship on this topic.

In her book *Eloquent Rage*, Brittney Cooper[1] wrote in a chapter entitled "White-Girl Tears" about how Black women grow up being denied the protection of femininity that White women are afforded. Cooper observed that "White girls usually cry white-lady tears after they have done something hella racist and then been called out by the offended party for doing so. To shift blame and claim victimhood, they start to cry. The world falls apart as people rush to their defense."[2]

Cooper talks about her and others' experiences of racialized aggression toward them at the hands of White women during public lectures as well as everyday interactions on campus. She also reflects on the long history of the lengths that White men will go to defend the narrative of vulnerable White femininity, such as threatening to kill Ida B. Wells for her investigative reports of false claims of rape of White women from Black men.[3] This kind of response reifies a culture in which White women can call upon the dominant narrative to support and center Whiteness through femininity.

However, in embracing the complexities of race and gender, Cooper also notes that the tears of Dr. Christine Blasey Ford were legitimate tools to use against patriarchy. Cooper shared at a national conference on women that during the Kavanaugh hearings she was relying on the power of "White girl tears," and she needed Christine Blasey Ford to be heard and believed. According to Cooper, Dr. Blasey Ford is a most upstanding White woman— well educated, from a particular class of White folks, and very poised; "and yet, those white men trounced all over her like she was standing in their way as they sought to get the keys to the kingdom, which she kind of was."[4] Cooper went on to reflect that what she hoped White women learned from the Kavanaugh hearings was the lesson that, you cannot get in bed with White supremacy without also getting in bed with patriarchy. Cooper once also lamented in a panel discussion: "The things that I knew already as a Black woman in America, is that if white women's tears cannot compel any kind of moral compunction for white men, what does that mean for the rest of us?"[5]

Tears from White women can serve as the trump card specifically when conversations on race become heated. Humans are socialized to respond to tears, which are often the first sign for everyone in a given situation to pause, wait, inquire, and give time for the individual to gather and compose. Tears often center the crier—and thus the person who appears to be hurt last has the most power in the moment. Equity scholars have recognized and highlighted how tears have become weaponized.

A 2018 article in *The Guardian* by Ruby Hamad was simply, yet profoundly, entitled "How white women use strategic tears to silence women of colour."[6] Hamad makes the argument that White women have effectively silenced the legitimate grievances of Black and other women of color with their "damsel in distress" emotive responses to pain. Hamad writes,

> Trauma assails brown and black women from all directions. There is the initial pain of being subjected to gendered racism and discrimination, there is the additional distress of not being believed or supported, and of having your words and your bravery seemingly credited to others.[7]

Blogger Awesomely Luvvie[8] writes that White women have been weaponizing their tears to divert and subvert Black pain, and their tears are effective. Luvvie submits that the tears of White women are "especially potent and extra salty because they are tantamount to femininity."[9] White tears are a powerful form of White static. They redirect the focus from racial justice issues onto a form of crumbling femininity, an already heightened sensitivity in the culture of White supremacy. Though the physical tears of White women may be genuine, they can serve to create further static to mask the understanding of pain for people of color in a seemingly inconspicuous way.

White Static of Allies

White allyship is in many ways the most prominent display of White static used to exonerate oneself from the complicity of systemic racism. This line of thinking fits well with the ideology of individualism that is part of White western North American culture.

In 1963, jailed civil rights activist Martin Luther King, Jr. voiced a concern with White moderates. In his famous *Letter from a Birmingham Jail*, Dr. King outlined his concerns plainly:

> First, I must confess that over the past few years I have been gravely disappointed with the white moderate. I have almost reached the regrettable conclusion that the Negro's great stumbling block in his stride toward freedom is not the White Citizen's

Counciler or the Ku Klux Klanner, but the white moderate, who is more devoted to "order" than to justice; who prefers a negative peace which is the absence of tension to a positive peace which is the presence of justice; who constantly says: "I agree with you in the goal you seek, but I cannot agree with your methods of direct action"; who paternalistically believes he can set the timetable for another man's freedom; who lives by a mythical concept of time and who constantly advises the Negro to wait for a "more convenient season." Shallow understanding from people of good will is more frustrating than absolute misunderstanding from people of ill will. Lukewarm acceptance is much more bewildering than outright rejection.[10]

Dr. King's concern over racism was not limited to overtly racist categories. Instead, he pointed out the insidiousness of racism hidden in White liberalism. This subliminal nature is a significant element of systemic racism.

Blogger and public theologian, Ally Henny, recently reflected on the problem of White liberals being the biggest challenge. What she offers is in many ways the bookend to Dr. King's critique of White moderates:

Most assuredly, the most difficult and dangerous white people to those of us in antiracism work are not the gradualists, the moderates, the neophytes, or even the unapologetic racists .... [T]he white "ally" who thinks they're farther along than they are is dangerous because they often become wolves in sheep's clothes. They refuse to listen when called out. They have an excuse for their toxic actions .... They've built a "brand" and see themselves as being unimpeachable because certain people might endorse them. The truth is that they think they've arrived when they haven't even left home.[11]

This sense of allyship is a manifestation and fruit of White static used by White people to distance themselves from systemic racism. If one of the biggest fears for White people is being called the r[word], then one of the biggest hopes of White liberals is to be called an ally. They consider themselves "woke" and often strive for a Black pat. An ally is generally thought of as someone in the dominant group who identifies as an advocate on behalf of an oppressed population. The motivation to be an ally is an important part of the equation. There is a fundamental difference between someone who is learning to participate in solidarity, and someone who believes she already knows how to help—or who is in possession of White truth. Allyship then becomes yet another manifestation of Whitefluenza. The desire to be identified as an ally based on limited knowledge and experience and without suffering the costs because of ones allyship actually demonstrates a greater pursuit of privilege.

This sense of arrival means that the systemic and corporate nature of racism and a lack of personal benefits for the ally poses a problem. So do the ideas of charity, *noblesse oblige*, and a messianic savior mentality. Ally Henny acutely articulates being leery of people who:

- Are always eager to educate but don't ever seem to be learning anything new.
- Always have something to say, but don't listen to others when they speak ...
- Put themselves in the position to try to speak on issues of black and brown people in their communities, but haven't done work on their own toxic whiteness ...
- Treat black and brown folks like thought experiments. In other words, when they want to intellectualize, pontificate, and debate about what they think about racism but don't want to be told if or why they're wrong.[12]

The desire to be named an ally—cited in the work, but rarely ever doing the work—creates a high degree of static that drowns out the real issues at hand.

The White Static of Bootstrap Ideology

Bootstrap ideology is a common and fallacious line of reasoning character-ized by the thinking: "work hard and pull yourself up by your bootstraps." The ideology presupposes that the problem with lack of mobility for people of color is not a systemic issue but rather a question of individual hard work and effort. This, of course, is problematic because it assumes that everyone already possesses bootstraps by which to pull themselves up. Indeed, this is an implicit and racially charged idea that is lurking in the background of the White playbook, but it is not new. It is, however, an essential argument in defending White dominance.

Hillbilly Elegy[13] is a memoir by J. D. Vance about growing up poor in Appalachia. The book played a prominent role in Whitesplaining the rise of Trump and the discontent embedded in White America and in perpetuating a colorblind depiction of poverty. The book was not a reaction to Trump, but circumstantially emerged as a way to understand why poverty in White America combines with political ideology and religion to perpetuate the belief that the straight White Christian male is the most oppressed class in the United States.

Vance's story is the ultimate "I hurt, too" response to all the perceived White-male bashing from America's liberals and people of color. In his book, Vance indicates that race and ethnicity are in the background of his argument. He claims that the racial frame has been *overplayed* as a way to explain difference in the United States. If poverty is colorblind and White people can overcome their circumstances, *then so should any other group*. This line of logic reveals a bootstrap ideology. The first step to believing wealth is colorblind is to believe that poverty is colorblind.

My (Collins) great-great-grandfather, James Ervin Tomlin, fought for the south in the Civil War and was captured twice. He married Cordelia Clementine Clines. Her nickname was *tar pitch and turpentine* because, according to our family history, she smoked and dipped tobacco at the same time. They lived in rural Alabama, and I grew up visiting the land they lived and worked on and the places where my grandparents, parents, cousins, aunts, and uncles were raised. My family history is laced with violence, substance abuse, poverty, and manual labor. I understand the argument and appeal of *Hillbilly Elegy*. However, dating back to the Civil War, through Jim Crow and civil rights, to Confederate flags flying and being worn on the heads of my cousins, to a constant use of the n[word], and a perpetual questioning of how many Black kids were in my class as a child, one thing is clear—race was always and is part of any hillbilly's *elegy*. Any attempt to extract race from that narrative is an attempt to enhance White dominance. Growing up poor but being White, as is the case for J.D. Vance, or being gay and White, as was the case for Jennifer Hart (see Chapter 3), serve as proxies for jamming the signal of racial consciousness by offering substitutes for White dominance and racial inequities. White static.

The spawn of White noise is White silence. Not having an answer and saying nothing out of fear is revealing. White students and colleagues we have interacted with have Whitesplained their silence with statements like, "I'm not gonna say anything at all, because I don't want to sound or look racist." We do not want you to sound less racist. We want you to *become* anti-racist.

White Echo

The importance of understanding the echo effect of White noise lies in the propagation of White dominance beyond the container of a White body. In social settings and organizations, those who were previously powerless may repeat the same power-holding behaviors of those who had power over them in a hierarchy. White echo is a term that helps excavate the ways in which White dominance manifests within people of color, but the focus is on the oppressive origin of the noise as opposed to those who are just the echo.

The White Echo of Kanye

White echoes reverberate across politics, entertainment, education, and religion. In a conversation with President Trump in the Oval Office in January 2019, where Kanye West was supposed to address crime in Chicago, the rap artist presented a succession of apparently non-sequitur comments about the prison system, economics, racism, and patriotism. He talked about the problem of Black-on-Black crime, stating that in his community, Black people are killing each other more than the police were. West, wearing a red Make America Great Again (MAGA) hat, sat across from the president, and shared how the "MAGA" slogan made him feel powerful. Kanye stated that whenever he put on the MAGA hat, "It made me feel like Superman."[14] This is the same Kanye West who at one point in his career criticized then-president George W. Bush, saying he did not care about Black people after the president's mishandling of Hurricane Katrina. Old Kanye's rap songs exposed social issues such as police brutality, violence in Chicago, and Black activism. New Kanye is an example of the White echo. He is not alone. The motivations for his actions are not completely clear, but in a recent interview with David Letterman, he spoke about being bipolar as being akin to having a sprained brain, and the social response to his disorder akin to having his throat stepped on. Kanye's echoes are not just about his personal motivations, but provide a gateway for examining White ideologies.

Frantz Fanon, depicting a White person speaking to a Black person, wrote: "'I know Black people; you have to talk to them kindly, talk to them about their country; knowing how to talk to them, that's the key. Now here's what you do …'"[15] He went on to emphasize that this type of rhetoric is no exaggeration, and that a "white man talking to a person of color behaves exactly like a grown-up with a little kid, simpering, murmuring, fussing, and coddling."[16] West exemplified a twist on Fanon's description; but West was using Black vernacular, was in the White house wearing a red hat, and articulated the White dominant ideology of a racist, sexist, homophobic president. Trump played the role of coddling the White echo in Kanye West. Economic viability and power represent one form of privilege. There is a fine line between the oppressor and the oppressed. As Freire stated, the oppressed become the hosts of the oppressor.[17]

In what was perhaps a prophetic statement, West talked about the courage that came from the red hat. Hearken back to the image and discussion of young Nick Sandmann in the chapter on White pain, when we posed the question, smirk or smile? Based on Kanye West's assertion that red caps are tantamount to red capes in terms of courage, one might agree that the caps are indeed an impetus that leads to empowerment. People of any race can feel emboldened to speak up and speak out to reclaim an imagined White-dominated America.

The White Echo of Tiger

The 2019 Masters Golf Tournament victory went to Tiger Woods, who after a long drought from winning a major championship made what many in the sports broadcasting business would call a comeback. Shortly after his victory, President Trump draped a medal around Tiger Woods' neck in a White House ceremony for the Presidential Medal of Freedom (for context, Rush Limbaugh was also awarded the same medal at the 2020 State of the Union address). At the ceremony, President Trump said to the 2019 Master's winner: "Tiger, we are inspired by everything you've become and attained. The job you've done is incredible." Trump continued, "Your spectacular achievements on the golf course, your triumph over physical adversity and your relentless will to win, win, win; these qualities embody the American spirit of pushing boundaries, defying limits and always striving for greatness."

Prior to the event, Woods was asked about his relationship with Trump, and he said, "He's the president of the United States. You have to respect the office. No matter who is in the office, you may like, dislike personality or the politics, but we all must respect the office."[18] None of these comments, nor his visit to the White House are problematic in and of themselves. However, it is his race avoidance with media, as well as his respect of an office held by a racist president that is the problem. The official announcement of the medal uses language to refer to Tiger as something he refuses to call himself—Black. In contrast, Warriors head coach Steve Kerr and the Warriors team, made up of mostly Black athletes, refused to visit the White House after winning the 2017 NBA championship. Countless other athletes and coaches refused to visit President Trump in solidarity with racial equity activists.

Tiger has been controversial in some Black communities (and to a lesser extent the Thai communities) over his racial identity because he publicly stated that he was not Black.[19] Gary Younge critiqued Tiger Woods in a piece in *The Guardian* for missing the opportunity to embrace Blackness. Younge referenced an Oprah Winfrey interview when Woods was asked whether it bothered him being referred to as African-American, to which Woods responded that it did bother him. He went on to identify himself as a 'Cablinasian'—a mix of Caucasian, Black, Indian and Asian. Younge further criticized Woods, saying that his resistance to identify as Black "represented not an advance but a retreat in our efforts to retire race as a restrictive category. For far from abolishing racial categories by coining 'Cablinasian', he simply created a whole new category just for himself."[20] As Woods collected his medal, so did Mr. Trump—meaning that hanging a medal around the neck of a person of color became a token, a trophy, a mark of accomplishment for a president who has emboldened White nationalism.

The infighting among communities of color, and the tokenism that some people of color participate in and benefit from, should not be the exclusive responsibility of the minoritized group. Whose fault is this? Perhaps the easiest and most convenient reaction is to vilify Woods and West as sellouts. This however plays right into the individualistic nature of White ideology and breeds tokenism, moving the critique away from systemic problems. White echoes reverberate and are personified through Black, Brown, and Asian bodies. Critical racial consciousness requires an evolutionary disposition. One must excavate the *origins* of the White supremacist logic and rhetoric—not demonize the echo. By focusing on the noise, rather than on the noise maker, one can see the structural ways in which the echo is derived from a system of White supremacy.

The Reverend Jesse Jackson once shared the following remarks that epitomize the White echo: "There is nothing more painful to me at this stage in my life than to walk down the street and hear footsteps and start thinking about robbery—then look around and see somebody white and feel relieved."[21] This is the conundrum of racial consciousness. He was preaching a message that was geared toward being tough on crime. Jackson's sentiment became an echo of Whiteness for many who may have felt validated that a Black person would finally state what many non-Black citizens were feeling.

Andrew Yang, a failed democratic candidate for the 2020 presidential election, made waves with self deprecating jokes about being an Asian who is good at math. His comments received mixed reactions. While a mostly White audience found such commentary humorous, Yang received criticism from Asian American activists who expressed frustration with the perpetuation of an old racist stereotype. The extenuation of the model minority myth serves the interests of White power structures.

It is a convolution of representation and voice for communities of color. Yang's humor and Jackson's comments have driven a wedge into relationships, politics, and equity advocacy efforts. White echoes are words, concepts, and voices representing a dominant group that are embodied and perpetuated by both White people as well as people of color.

White Amplifiers

A third and final concept for White noise involves the idea of *White amplifiers*. In a musical performance, it is essential that amplifiers are built around a soundboard. Soundboards in musical instruments help to amplify the original sound of a given instrument. In the case of the piano, a soundboard is the thin wooden board underneath the strings. This board is what gives a piano its incredible power and sustainable tone. In the music industry and the audiovisual world, amplification is perfected via the mixing board, a console that sound engineers use to match the levels of the inputs from singers' microphones, accompaniment of orchestral instruments, and other plug-in electric instruments. Amplification is especially critical in speeches and public addresses, so they may be heard loud and clear.

Just as well-engineered amplification is the key to clear and audible sound in a performance, so *White amplification* comprises the construction of a message engineered and perfected to ensure that listeners catch the correct tone, tenor, and intended content. All of the sound that hits a listening audience has been intentionally designed and directed by the engineer.

We make a distinction between a White echo and a White amplifier. Unlike an echo, an amplifier works to enhance rather than just mimic the original note. Echoes may dissipate the farther is strays from the original source. Amplifers project the tone even at greater distances from the source. The echo is intended to replicate White ideologies while the amplifier goes a step further to expand White ideology on a deeper lever; even creating original content to perpetuate White supremacy. We argue that some people of color have unwittingly become White amplifiers to carry forward the tunes created by the original source.

Examples of amplifers can be found throughout history. In Europe during World War II, Nazi sympathizers who were Jewish oversaw their own people, complying with the will of their Nazi oppressors. In the Pacific Rim, Japanese imperialists found ethnic Koreans to serve as overseers of other colonized Koreans, holding crucial roles as enforcers to keep law and order and maintain the Empire of Japan. The role of the Black overseer was also documented in the U.S. during the days of chattel slavery, and racial epithets such as "Uncle Tom" emerged within the Black community to describe enslaved people who perpetuated the power imbalance by policing their own communities. In some of these instances, the overseers and sympathizers created their own rules to inflict pain horizontally and oppress their own people. These are examples of amplifiers that enhance and sustain the dominant message of the colonizer.

In the realm of politics, White amplifiers are tokenized and minoritized peoples who amplify the rhetoric in a way that makes the plight of people of color seem unrealistic or diminished. The amplification becomes a powerful form of gaslighting. Senators Ted Cruz and Marco Rubio are examples of Latinx Republican presidential candidates who epitomize White amplifiers. Ted Cruz made an accolade about a formidable opponent of Martin Luther King Jr. and Civil Rights, saying the senate would benefit from having "100 more like Jesse Helms." Neither Cruz nor Rubio are willing to denounce the rhetoric and tweets from the Trump campaign as racist, nor are they willing to advocate against policies that demonize and criminalize people who are Latinx.

One example of a White amplifer in higher education is an affirmative action lawsuit against Harvard University. The president of the special interest group Students for Fair Admissions (SFFA) is Edward Blum, and he has repeatedly sought ideal cases to dismantle race-concious admission. After several failed, yet tenacious attempts with White students (see the cases with Abigail Fisher against UT Austin), he turned his attention to Asian Americans and Harvard. Blum sought to perpetuate the myth that Harvard's racial balancing was discriminatory against Asian Americans and therefore insight ire against race conscious admission.

During the campaign, over sixty Asian American groups (c.f., the Asian American Coalition on Education) signed on to Blum's agenda. By perpetuating the victim status of a minoritized group, the White logic agenda of eradicating race conscious admission was amplified. The White logic was quickly embraced, embodied, and perpetuated by Asian American groups who made the ideology their own. To focus on the Asian American groups and pit them against other minoritized groups is problematic in that it ignores the origin of the noise and only focuses on the amplification.

Faulty and racialized concepts, like the "model minority myth," have historically been thrust upon the Asian American communities to pit one ethnic group against another.[22] Some sub-groups of East Asian American students have been highlighted by the media to demonstrate that the academic prowess of *all* Asian Americans that ought to be emulated by other ethnic groups. The problem is that both White people and people of color, including some Asian Americans, have bought into the model minority myth. What exacerbates this stereotype of the Asian American model minority myth is that some academic and economic success has in fact been true for some Asian Americans. As Nigerian author Chimamanda Adichie stated, "the problem with stereotypes is not that they are untrue, but that they are incomplete. They make one story become the only story."[23] Asian Americans have been baited as minorities to unwittingly amplify and support the narrative of the dominant White majority. There is no better example of a White amplifier than those who embody the model minority myth to help perpetuate a dominant White ideology.

Duality and Tension for People of Color

Most educational institutions in America have mission statements and diversity statements that have emerged from hours of painfully endured departmental or university-wide retreats. For some institutions, the end result will be the creation of a diversity office and/or the position of chief diversity officer (CDO). It is a worthy effort. However, what inevitably happens is that the chief diversity officer role becomes something much more symbolic. Like being professionally ethnic. The CDO role often exists to ensure that all the ethnic students feel welcome. What this position should include, however, is the authority to lead institutional or systemic change, instead of merely asking students of color to adapt at dominant White institutions. Chief diversity officers can become chief absolution officers.

Another side of a chief absolution officer is the role of *chief overseer*. In what may be the modern-day academic plantation, a president, provost, or dean may send in a chief diversity officer to quell an increasingly restless minority student group on the brink of chaos, in a desperate attempt to avoid a sit-in, a hunger strike, or another campus escalation. In any scenario, this chief diversity officer is stuck between a rock and a hard place. This is a unique burden for the CDO. While chief diversity officers may be openly hired to coordinate diversity efforts on college campuses, they also live in the tension of being asked to mollify fellow colleagues of color.

Beyond the CDO universities also have people of color in a variety of academic and administrative positions. While their job descriptions have nothing to do with diversity, their reality is that there are unwritten duties to provide feedback, support, and mentoring to improve racial climate. These educators often feel the burden of unspoken expectations for any diversity work that emerges on campus. Such uncompensated dual appointments for people of color represent additional labor. For example, faculty of color might be asked to serve on a diversity committee or council, in order to provide compositional diversity and speak on behalf of people of color. They will invariably have conversations with White colleagues about diversity, and they might also be mentoring younger emerging scholars, administrators, and students of color who are thrilled to see someone who looks like them. Educators of color then become diversity ambassadors on campus.

Consequently, for many faculty of color, their *visible* appointment requires competent teaching in their specialization; while at the same time their *invisible* appointment requires additional instructional responsibilities. They will likely be successful in the visible appointment, but their passion may slowly decay and die, because of the invisible appointment. There is a tax upon the soul of a person whose daily professional responsibility is really two jobs. Moreover, educators of color are financially compensated for only one of these dual appointments.

Part of the challenge of addressing the Whiteness of any institution is that its White noise was never intended as a conspiracy, but is the uncritical and unintentional byproduct of a White architecture of the mind. It creates real challenges to the mental and physical health of people of color. Many colleagues of color at universities across the country have shared with us just how tired they are. Many of them come limping into the workshops we offer, exhausted from dealing with the White noise of the racialized conversations, frustrated by the ceaseless racial incidents on campus, and flabbergasted that they must explain to White colleagues, yet again, the significance of racialized events around the country. They have learned to mourn privately over the deaths of Black and Brown children, because experience has taught them that to do so publicly only leads to more debates that leave them even more tired, yet still grieving.

A conversation that I (Jun) have had with a handful of colleagues of color, mostly Asian Americans, has revolved around our abilities to navigate White spaces and cultures, and interact with White people. Sociologists refer to this as code-switching.

In one particular group text celebrating news of a merit-based increase, one Asian American friend wrote: "How were you able to get such a big raise this year? You must have mad *White game*"—which led to a plethora of happy face and thumbs up emojis as well as replies such as "Don't hate the player, hate the game!" White game then, is the skill that people of color have recognized, developed and mastered in order to navigate White spaces successfully. I have half-jokingly stated to some of my junior colleagues and emerging Korean-American professionals that the secret to success in America is essentially to "act White"—in other words develop your White game.

I have often stated that you can take Alex out of Korea but you can never take Korea out of Alex. In other words, generations of culture are passed down to me, and I unwittingly accept them as part of my own value system. For me, it has often meant that I choose to not be my authentic self in White dominant spaces. My Korean-American heritage and culture relies on the proper honor and respect of my elders and deference (demonstrated by not looking people in the eyes, for example) to those I am subordinate to. This is often interpreted by a dominant White majority as timidity, servility, and a lack of confidence, and thus often not leadership material.

Publicly sharing these types of secret or private conversations I have had with other non-White friends is risky. How might my White friends handle this type of discussion if I were to introduce these topics in conversation? Among some of my friends of color, we have sometimes talked about the concept of being an effective communicator to White people. I have heard the expression *White whisperer* used in a complimentary fashion in reference to certain equity educators of color, for their ability to have "real talk" with White people without having them walk away upset, offended, or defensive. White whisperer is meant as a compliment, to be sure, for being both winsome in content and tone. Using self-deprecating humor, maintaining a posture of calm introspection and being responsive with empathetic ears to the initial "I hurt, too" responses from White people working through difficult conversations. These are just some of the hallmarks of a White whisperer that help facilitate White learning. "You are just so easy to listen to, not like some others who have talked about race in the past ... some of them are just too angry and I cannot hear them through the anger and emotion," someone once shared with me after a lengthy conversation on racism. On the one hand, being a White whisperer is ideal for a race and equity educator because of the ability to keep people at the table. On the other hand, the term can be perceived as a pejorative by educators of color for re-centering Whiteness, White feelings, and White fragility in an already White-dominated space.

Unscrambling White Noise

I (Jun) have a confession. I have not been consistent in my annual checkups with my primary care physician. I am about a dozen years older than my co-author (Collins). The last time I went, my physician told me that I was not getting any younger. She also added that I certainly was getting heavier, and that weight gain could pose a potential problem for me in later years. So, my physician recommended diet and exercise. She also suggested a change in my thinking about what I want to eat, so I would begin making healthier food choices and the like. My annual physical examination concluded with a stern warning from her, that if I did not deal with this now, my health could deteriorate.

I agree with my physician—in theory. But she is asking me to put effort into something challenging, and my response is that the recommendation sounds both difficult and expensive. You want me to join a gym and buy healthier foods? You want me to cook my own food, not buy processed fried foods, and not eat at McDonald's anymore? That sounds expensive. Again, I agree with her in theory, but the application of this is going to be very difficult. Are there other options?

When I travel to other campuses and talk to colleagues about dismantling White supremacy and the ever-pressing dangers of systemic racism, most people have responded to me with a variation of the following: "Dr. Jun, I can agree with you—in theory. While I have understood what you have shared and understand your recommendations, if we were to make all these changes you are suggesting, it would be difficult, very expensive, unpopular, and probably impossible. Are there other options?"

There is no quick fix or guaranteed method for success, whether for personal fitness or for anti-racism work. White supremacy is a complex problem that took generations to create; it will require a comprehensive solution that will be painful to implement and will take untold time to accomplish.

In one exchange, an institutional leader listened to our recommendations and replied, "Can we just do one thing, like make racial microaggressions go away in classrooms? If we can just get faculty to stop saying certain words in class, maybe that will fix the problem. Just help us to do and say the right things that will not come across as racist."

This institutional leader fundamentally failed to understand that our goal is never to make educators *sound* less racist; it was for them to *become* less racist. Consultation workshops and diversity classes were never meant to serve as finishing schools—even though sounding less racist, rather than being less racist, is a lot more efficient and seemingly economical. The problem and solution begin with an acknowledgment that a lot of work occurs in the interior. Sometimes behavioral change and external changes are necessary, but they lack the long-term systemic leverage of cultivating critical collective racial consciousness.

There is an ongoing debate about the priority of external versus internal or attitudes versus behavior. We have heard the criticism from our graduate students, as well as from participants at various workshops we have facilitated, that we only talk about White supremacy but do not offer any solutions. People who are the most anxious for action are oftentimes still the least conscious of the need to engage in interior, self-work. Part of the fixation with solutions may be attached to the fact that White people in positions of leadership are accustomed to solving problems—even other people's problems—more than they are required to examine their interior lives. At the same time, those who stop their work at the interior life fail to make connections to systemic issues.

Given the nature and intent of this book, we focus on examples of White spaces within interpersonal relationships. Sometimes, White people who may consider themselves allies and advocates for racial justice might limit their relevant conversations to interactions with people of color (seeking the ever-gratifying and elusive Black pat). However, when confronted by comments from White noise from family and friends, what is one to do? Do we address issues with colleagues and say nothing at home? This is the initial approach that I (Collins) took in my awakening stages of racial consciousness. Most conversations about issues of diversity occurred with people of color and rarely with other White folks. I certainly did not engage family or long-time friends with these conversations. I am still searching for ways to navigate the right time, place, and words to engage and to disrupt the White noise.

There is a collective frailty of the process of learning and communicating through difficult conversations. We are imperfect and incomplete in our motivations and our attempts to dialogue. Often, we say too much or too little, but we strive to be humble and always evolving. Learning how to do this right takes time and a great deal of practice. This is where understanding the concept of White noise can be useful. Ask the question, how does racial dominance obscure a perspective, ideology, or rhetoric? Does the rhetoric or logic send a message intended to obscure or scramble the perspective of another racial lens? Furthermore, how can dominance manifest itself in ally behavior and recreate another layer of White static? Finding and identifying these logics in institutional norms, individual behaviors, and in political rhetoric is a first step in unscrambling the message.

Addressing the manifestation of Whiteness in people of color is a risk. White echoes and White amplifiers are very complex manifestations of White supremacy because they come through in people of color. White folks can take discussions like these and misappropriate them in ways that fit into another White supremacist logic. Our purpose, however, is to address White supremacy wherever it exists, and to acknowledge that it goes beyond White bodies. The work of consciousness by Frantz Fanon, double consciousness by W. E. B. Du Bois, and the statement by Cornel West, "I am trying to kill the White supremacist in me," all stay with us and inform our belief that critical racial consciousness is a struggle. Workshops, college courses, and guest speakers on diversity are often perceived as being directed at White people personally, but in reality, they are directed at White supremacy.

Anyone openly committed toward fighting the immense proliferation of White supremacist logic and violence, but not also willing to excavate the manifestations of White supremacy in their own mental framework, is not using all of the tools required to dismantle systemic oppression in our society. The most difficult aspect of cultivating a critical racial consciousness is to look in the mirror and examine the ways in which the oppressive structure has found its way into our psyche. Identifying and filtering out the examples of White noise is a key component of the way the White logic comes through both stealth and overt ways in politics, education, and other areas of the public sphere. Unscrambling and decoding the script behind White noise will help to reconstruct the logic system to evolve toward a collective critical racial consciousness.

Notes

1. Cooper, Brittney. *Eloquent Rage: One Black Feminists Refusal to Bow Down*. St. Martins Press, 2018.
2. Ibid, p. 172.

3. Ibid.
4. "NowThis Politics." NowThis Politics—Scholar Brittney Cooper: Kavanaugh Hearings Exposed the Ties between White Supremacy and Patriarchy to White Women #WITW. Accessed May 16, 2019. https://www.facebook.com/NowThisPolitics/videos/303178037017407/.
5. Ibid.
6. Hamad, Ruby. "How White Women Use Strategic Tears to Silence Women of Colour | Ruby Hamad." *The Guardian*. May 07, 2018. Accessed April 22, 2019. https://www.theguardian.com/commentisfree/2018/may/08/how-white-women-use-strategic-tears-to-avoid-accountability.
7. Ibid.
8. Awesomely Luvvie. "About the Weary Weaponizing of White Women Tears." *Awesomely Luvvie*. April 23, 2018. Accessed April 22, 2019. https://www.awesomelyluvvie.com/2018/04/weaponizing-white-women-tears.html.
9. Ibid.
10. King, Martin Luther. 1968. "Letter from a Birmingham Jail." [Atlanta, Ga.]: Martin Luther King Jr. Center for Nonviolent Social Change.
11. Ally Henny. Ally Henny—Most Assuredly, the Most Difficult and … Accessed May 16, 2019. https://www.facebook.com/allyhennypage/posts/1216048481878793?sfnsw=cl.
12. Ibid.
13. Vance, James David. *Hillbilly Elegy: A Memoir of a Family and Culture in Crisis*. New York: Harper, 2018.
14. France, Lisa Respers. "New Year, Same Old Kanye Love for Trump." *CNN*. January 02, 2019. Accessed May 07, 2019. https://www.cnn.com/2019/01/02/entertainment/kanye-west-trump-tweets/index.html.
15. Fanon, Frantz, Charles Lam Markmann, Ziauddin Sardar, and Homi K. Bhabha. *Black Skin, White Masks*. London: Pluto, 2008. p. 14.
16. Ibid.
17. Freire, Paulo and Donaldo Macedo. *Pedagogy of the Oppressed*. New York: Bloomsbury Academic, 2018.
18. Chamberlain, Samuel. "Trump Presents 'True Legend' Tiger Woods with Presidential Medal of Freedom." *Fox News*. Accessed May 07, 2019. https://www.foxnews.com/sports/trump-tiger-woods-presidential-medal-of-freedom.
19. Jr., Stephen A. Crockett, and Stephen A. Crockett Jr. "I'm Not Black, I'm Tiger." *The Root*. April 15, 2019. Accessed May 17, 2019. https://www.theroot.com/i-m-not-black-i-m-tiger-1834050594.
20. Younge, Gary. "Tiger Woods: Black, White, Other | Racial Politics." *The Guardian*. May 28, 2010. Accessed June 04, 2019. https://www.theguardian.com/sport/2010/may/29/tiger-woods-racial-politics.
21. Herbert, Bob. "In America; A Sea Change On Crime." *The New York Times*. December 12, 1993. Accessed May 16, 2019. https://www.nytimes.com/1993/12/12/opinion/in-america-a-sea-change-on-crime.html.

22. "Asian Americans and Pacific Islanders—a FAQ." *NBCNews.com*. Accessed May 07, 2019. https://www.nbcnews.com/news/asian-america/asian-americans-pacific-islanders-faq-n998661?fbclid=IwAR0I99_6Ifyx6Bfh9iEjFG_WfxQQNUuL-x6weN4hRlX5E0cw69jwUOhmYg4.

23. Adichie, Chimamanda Ngozi. *TED*. Accessed May 07, 2019. https://www.ted.com/talks/chimamanda_adichie_the_danger_of_a_single_story?language=en.

· 8 ·

WHITE CONSCIOUSNESS: THE CONSTANT STRUGGLE

The cumulative impact of White pain, White 22, Whitefluenza, White wrath, and White noise ultimately works as a resounding defense of White dominance. There is a powerful force that operates in the White architecture of the mind, which seeks to White out whatever might expose the power of a system built on White logic. However, White logic can be deconstructed. White architecture can be redesigned. Whiteness can evolve with a collective critical racial consciousness.

There is a recognition for a need to reconstruct and evolve in racial consciousness. That recognition, however, is often in tension with the current power system that maintains the status quo. Therefore, the recognition is paradoxical. For example, even the U.S. Department of Justice has mandated implicit bias training for its employees. The Federal Bureau of Investigations, Drug Enforcement Administration, U.S. Marshalls, and U.S. attorneys, which has reached almost 30,000 federal personnel, have all attempted to implement some type of training.[1] These are examples of paradox.

We are exploring a means for evolving collective critical racial consciousness by recognizing that even where there is no *cure*, consciousness can be a form of remission. Consciousness requires the cultivation of constant awareness, engagement in the battle, developing strategy, and building up new strength, connections, and healthy behaviors. Since the book *White Out* was released in 2017, we have conducted numerous workshops, consultations, and book clubs. We compiled all of the feedback we received and developed this concept of *collective critical racial consciousness* to focus on specific systemic and individual considerations for readers to implement in their own spheres of influence. In their process of self-excavation, they can participate in systemic change.

Hegemony is defined as a "cultural power, including the dominant cultural patterns that achieve and sustain their dominance by encouraging—but not forcing—people to believe in them."[2] Hegemonic Whiteness is an identity that both produces and maintains domination through power and privilege.[3] Where Whiteness can be internalized as normative and natural, it can in turn mark non-White culture, behavior, and people as abnormal and unnatural. Positions of dominance and subordination thus are sustained, not necessarily by force, but through social practices, systems, and norms.[4] Systems of oppression are maintained because society does not challenge the validity of norms and attitudes that perpetuate systems of domination and subordination, simply because they are viewed as normal.[5]

Paolo Freire defines critical consciousness as learning to perceive and understand social, political, economic, and racial contradictions, and then act against the oppressive structures in our social reality. Without consciousness, the process of critical discovery is absent, and *with* consciousness the discovery that you have an oppressor status can cause strife; but this consciousness does not always lead to solidarity, which is a radical posture.[6]

A conversion away from this restricted perception "requires a profound rebirth," and those who go through it "must take on a new form of existence; they can no longer remain as they were."[7] The process of transformation provides a new awareness of reality and enhances the ability to recognize the logic and coding of power and oppression. Decoding this system then requires "moving from the part to the whole and then returning ... [and] requires that the Subject recognize himself in the object (the coded concrete existential situation)."[8] Individuals contribute to social realities which then contribute to the formation of individuals.

So, a *collective critical racial consciousness* can work on reconstructing reality *within* the ecosystem. This suggests that groups of individuals constantly struggling for racial consciousness can alter the social ecology. The excavation of our individual role within this reality leads to the interdependent recognition that "I cannot think *for others* or *without others*, nor can others think *for me*."[9] Self-excavation will move an individual away from a naïve approach to reality and into an ability to understand the root causes of oppression—that is, the architecture, logic, design, and sources of sustenance. Feelings of confusion and even disequilibrium can provoke a desire to unlearn supremacist behaviors. This can lead to a deeper critical racial consciousness in people who occupy dominant spaces.

The challenge of developing this type of consciousness, however, is the recognition that the individual is playing host to the oppressive structure, and then figuring out how to eliminate the oppressor from within. Franz Fanon describes his work with hope as a "mirror with a progressive infrastructure where the black man can find the path to disalienation."[10] In the same vein, we write in search of a collective critical racial consciousness toward a humanizing racial equity. Woven throughout White societies is a collective *unconscious*, which creates victims of White systems and perpetuates anti-Blackness. Achieving critical consciousness among White individuals is a daunting task; but herd immunity of the critical mass can protect society from the few who are either unwilling or unable.

As long as White privilege and supremacy remain veiled, systems of oppression will continue to reinforce the social power distance between racial identities.[11] People in the dominant group are granted unearned privileges, based upon the perception that membership belongs to those who possess certain characteristics and values related to that particular social group.[12] In Chapter 1 we presented several principles and conditions for an evolution toward racial justice that is predicated on cultivating critical racial consciousness. They include recognizing that:

1. Systems of power in society replicate inequality based on differences in race, gender, sexuality, ability, etc.
2. A mutual benefit exists whereby individual actions, behaviors, and ideologies need to be affirmed by a system, and they in turn perpetuate that system of supremacy.
3. Systems that perpetuate supremacy must be deconstructed and replaced with an ecosystem that relies on a deep interdependence for epistemological, physical, and spiritual survival.
4. There is no arrival point to being woke. White supremacy has a tenacious ability to regenerate and reappear in new ways, both individually and systemically. As a result, the work of eradicating such systems is *never* finished.

In an effort to explore the work of consciousness more deeply, we further examine the notions of root systems and their fruits, the function of mise-ducation in society, and the role of universities as carriers and sustainers of White logic and supremacy. Lastly, we emphasize that *White is not woke*—and that there is no past tense in the constant struggle for racial consciousness.

Roots and Fruits

In Chapter 2, we introduced the racial Rorschach test, which is essentially a strategy for decoding the logic system of Whiteness. When you see White supremacist violence by a man, is he a bad apple—an anomaly that is obscure and ultimately separate from society? Or is he part of the root system that is nourished by the education system, media, politics, religion, culture, and family history? When I (Jun) was living in Cambodia for a few years, I noticed how fertile the soil and the environment was. You could put a stick in the ground and it would sprout roots. But for some reason, the house we lived at did not have anything growing, in spite of all my efforts.

One day I brought home a bag of apples and taped each one of them to the barren tree in our yard. From a distance, the neighbors saw the fruit and said, "Congratulations!" My family saw what I was doing, realized my eccentricities were getting out of hand, and determined that it was time to return home to Los Angeles. What I did was *apple dangling*—trying to generate the desired results in a way that is disconnected from the root system (see Figure 8.1). Naturally, after just a short amount of time, the dangling apples rotted and fell away from the tree, as they were not tied to the life-giving source that cultivates the fruit from the roots.

Institutions often engage in apple dangling when working on diversity initiatives. Efforts to recruit people of color to the staff, faculty, or student body is essentially a kind of apple dangling. Root systems of institutions—their structure, context, and history—are rarely ever addressed. Diversity initiatives that are not tied to the life-giving source of the roots of the institution will inevitably end up with no fruitful results. The glossy programs or fresh new faces of people of color will rot and fall away from the tree; only this time, onlookers will see the rotten apples and likely place the blame on the fruit. Leaders at some institutions might sometimes intentionally leave those rotting dangling apples for all to see. This *strange fruit*[13] dangling from the tree would serve as a cautionary tale to others, and remind them of why quotas and affirmative action hires and other diversity fads do not work.

Figure 8.1: Roots and fruits, source Pixabay. https://pixabay.com/vectors/
tree-roots-fruits-grass-green-306092/

Institutional dialogues about diversity can be anxiety-inducing. A White person sitting in a diversity discussion may be bracing for somebody to accuse them of racism. I (Collins) am that straight White guy sitting in the meeting feeling nervous. Diversity is neither the problem nor the solution because both can be apple dangling. Racial justice must be rooted in racial consciousness, equity mindedness, and an active dismantling of White supremacy.

The corollary to apple dangling (influencing appearances without addressing the root structure) is the "bad apple" fallacy. When a fraternity is filmed reciting and singing racist chants, when a professor says the n[word] in class, when a student dresses in Blackface for Halloween (again), institutional authorities express shock and dismay because these actions do not represent the values (roots) of the institution. Or do they? When a White terrorist commits mass murder in a church, synagogue, or mosque, they are often characterized as mentally ill, deranged, or some other pathological label to distinguish them from the society (root system) in which they are embedded. In this way, they are identified as bad apples—random, isolated, anomalies that do not represent the whole. They are depicted as separate from the root system.

When it comes to apple dangling, there is rhetoric to manufacture fruits that are disconnected to the roots. When it comes to White supremacist violence, there is further rhetoric for *dis*connecting the fruit from the roots. However, we do not subscribe to the bad apple theory in either case. In a 2017 article in *Yes! Magazine* entitled "Stop using Mental Illness to Explain White Supremacy,"[14] Christopher Petrella and Justin Gomer argued that individualization reinforces the bad apple theory, and that structural White supremacy had become conflated with individual bigotry. This new narrative about mental illness ultimately offers a convenient way out for manifestations of White supremacy. They also submitted that

> [t]hose who continue to explain racial injustice through appeals to disease or illness implicitly reinforce a discourse that misdiagnoses the machinations of white supremacy. If we are truly to craft an antiracist politics capable of threatening the endurance of white supremacy, we must reject analyses and interventions that individualize social injustice by relying on notions of disease, mental illness, or deviance.[15]

Acts of racial violence are not manifestations of individual mental illness; rather, they are deeply connected to the ways in which society has nurtured hierarchy, supremacy, and racism.

Building on the imagery of roots and fruits, and keeping with an arboreal theme, consider the banyan and aspen trees. As societal roots relate to the individual, the analogy of the banyan tree is also applicable in a world full of White supremacy and anti-Blackness. The banyan tree is easily recognizable because of its exposed roots, which are indicators of a parasitic relationship that killed the original host. The banyan tree (Figure 8.2) begins as a seed that germinates in the host of another tree. As the seed grows, over time it actually takes over the host tree, and the extensive root system wraps around the limbs and trunk with enough force to kill the host, which then decomposes and leaves a hollow core.

Figure 8.3 shows aspen trees in Utah that grow in a root colony. New root stems can appear one hundred feet away from the parent, and this shared root system allows the colony to identically clone itself and also survive threats like forest fires—because even if a tree burns, the extensive shared root system will replenish the aspen forest. An aspen tree may only live one hundred years, but aspen colonies can live tens of thousands of years.

Each tree type has a unique root system, one of which is parasitic and the other a colonizing replicator. In much the same way, essential to White consciousness is an understanding of the ways in which our individual and societal root systems operate and replicate supremacy and oppression as opposed to racial equity and justice.

Figure 8.2: Banyan trees photo by author

In a eulogy delivered for four Black girls killed in a Birmingham church, Martin Luther King Jr. addressed the very nature of hatred, violence, and oppression rooted along racialized lines. In a poignant nod toward the power of systems and roots, he said, "We must be concerned not merely about who murdered them, but about the system, the way of life, the philosophy which produced the murderers."[16]

Figure 8.3: Aspen trees photo by author

Go Hitler!

In 2016, comedian and political commentator Trevor Noah[17] wrote an autobiography entitled *Born a Crime*. He was "born a crime" because he was born in South Africa to a White father and a Black mother. At the time, it was illegal for people of different races to marry or to have children, due to the influence of the Dutch Reformed Christian Church on the government. The country's laws were thus rooted in racism, miseducation, and a depraved Christian theology.

As Noah was growing up, he was educated in a system that was purposefully and intentionally distinct from White schools. Under apartheid, the Bantu education system was the only option for people who were not White—and it was a system designed to prepare students for the labor force. Accordingly, they did not learn history and math as the White students were learning it. Even so, the schools and other social structures required Black South Africans (Zulu, Xhosa, and several other people groups with distinct languages) to choose names that White people could pronounce. As a result, Noah literally had friends who were named Mussolini, Napoleon, Bruce Lee, and Hitler. They had no idea who some of these people were because they were not taught comprehensive histories, but they took on those names because they had heard them before and they saw the look on White people's faces upon hearing the names.

In the township where he lived, Noah and his friends had a variety of ways of finding entertainment, one of which was working as a DJ and dance crew. They learned to spin music and they learned to dance. The group began receiving invitations from White schools, sometimes to be the main entertainment or the token "cultural group" from the township. A White suburban school asked Noah and his dance crew to come and perform for their event. At the peak moment of their performance, they were playing music and dancing, and he said, "Here it comes." This was the biggest moment of their show. He said to the crowd, "Are you ready?" The crowd said, "Yes, we're ready!" He said, "No, no, no. You're not loud enough. Are you ready?" They're cheering wildly. Everybody was amped and excited.

He said, "Are you ready for HIIIITLEERRRRRRR!? Go Hitler! Go Hitler! Go Hitler!" The whole crew came out and their best dancer, Hitler, hit the floor and started dancing. The crowd, however, went dead silent. Noah was thinking, what's their problem? A woman came running out of the audience and said in her Afrikaner accent saying "How dare you? This is disgusting! You horrible, disgusting, vile creature! How *dare* you!!" While Noah was thinking, "What's your problem, lady?" She yelled at him, "You disgusting people!" and "My people have defeated you before and will defeat you again!" He heard her comments and understood the words to be couched in the context of White racist rhetoric of apartheid South Africa, and so the crew cursed the woman and packed up and left.

Unbeknownst to Noah, they were performing at a Jewish school. When the teacher said "my people," she was referring to Jewish people, and the offense was taken to the chanting of "Hitler." So, who was at fault in this encounter? Is it right to stand up in front of a Jewish audience and say, "Go Hitler?" Is it right to say to a multiracial black South African, "My people have defeated you before, we'll defeat you again?"

Whose fault is it? This is a question that vexes those who seek to place blame or who long for individual solutions to what is a complex systemic problem that has metastasized over time. We implore you to read or listen to Trevor Noah's book. When you read this story, how does the architecture of your mind program you to process the information? How do you decode the logic that undergirds the anecdote? It is another racial Rorschach test—do you see a smile or smirk?

The fruit of the scenario is a clash between race and identity, but the context and history indicate that the fault lies in the root system. In the case of South Africa, Bantu education was structural and intentional *miseducation*, and it hurt everyone in the society. The lingering impact of that miseducation will go on for generations and have a multiplier effect—one of which is White folks being miseducated to not understand history, context, and systemic racism. Miseducation of anyone is another path of evolution toward maintaining hierarchy and supremacy.

South Africa is a place full of dichotomy and tension. On a 2014 trip to South Africa our group of doctoral students and faculty were advised to eat at a famous place called Mzoli's, which is in the Gugulethu township outside of Cape Town. It is a place where patrons choose their meat and it is placed on the BBQ in the back. Once the meat is finished, it is brought out in metal bowls along with pap (coarsely ground maize similar to polenta) and chakalaka (a mix of tomatoes, onions, and peppers). It is a kind of street food, and is typically eaten by hand. We arrived there with our group and the driver (a White Afrikaner) would not get out of the minibus. He looked disgusted and uncomfortable. We asked if we could bring him some food—he balked and in his thick Afrikaner accent said, "I don't eat that dog food." It was easy in the moment to return the disgust toward the bus driver, and blame him for his ignorance and racism. It is harder to look back and think about the system that miseducated him and generated seeds of hatred that has lasted for generations. It is easier to blame a single piece of rotten fruit of apartheid—it is harder to examine and understand not only the roots that produced it, but also the soil, the water, the sources of survival and propagation. Racial consciousness requires an evolution from focusing on the single fruit to the systemic roots of miseducation, disgust, hatred, and supremacy.

Universities as Incubators of White Supremacy

White dominance has been engineered in the form of legitimated and codified knowledge. The Western European-North American continuum of formal science as the canon of human progress has delegitimized other forms of knowing in the world and designated White logic as enlightened. Phrenology and eugenics are overtly racist "sciences" that were cultivated in university settings in the past, but the same logic systems undergird many physical sciences and social sciences that are viewed in the contemporary academy as objective.

Donald Yacovone, an associate at the Hutchins Center for African and African American Research at Harvard University, conducted a thorough review of textbooks produced by university scholars to account for the ways in which the academy not only produces but diffuses White supremacist ideas. In spite of the fact that people often joke about the irrelevance of scholarship (and professors emphasize that relatively few people read their work), Yacovone's inquiry into Harvard's 3,000 history books from 1800–1980 tells a different story. After initially wading into the vast amount of resources, he reflected:

> I realized precisely what I was seeing, what instruction, and what priorities were leaping from the pages into the brains of the students compelled to read them: white supremacy. One text even began with the capitalized title: "The White Man's History." Across time and with precious few exceptions, African-Americans appeared only as "ignorant negroes," as slaves, and as anonymous abstractions that only posed "problems" for the supposed real subjects of history: white people of European descent. The assumptions of white priority, white domination, and white importance underlie every chapter and every theme of the thousands of textbooks that blanketed the country. This is the vast tectonic plate that underlies American culture. And while the worst features of our textbook legacy may have ended, the themes, facts, and attitudes of supremacist ideologies are deeply embedded in what we teach and how we teach it.[18]

Like the nineteenth-century eugenicists, phrenologists, social scientists, and psychologists who created proxies for racism and classism like "feeble-mindedness," these White historians were university-trained PhDs from places like the University of Chicago and the University of California, Berkeley. History books contain the genealogy of our disciplines, our knowledge, and our research methods. The roots of this genealogy have produced real fruits—like the fact that only 8% of high school students surveyed could identify slavery as the cause of the Civil War (even our history classes in California and Texas focused on the rights of states as the primary cause).[19] Miseducation.

The idea of racial science as part of the educational foundations of higher education in the United States has been well researched and documented by historian Craig Steven Wilder in his book, *Ebony and Ivy*.[20] In one chapter entitled "On the bodily and mental inferiority of the negro," Wilder recounts the 1808 trial of the *Commissioners of the Almshouse v. Alexander Whistelo*. Whistelo was Black man who was at the center of a paternity trial that evolved into a historic court case determining the nature of race. Whistelo had allegedly fathered a child with a mixed race/mulatto woman, but the child turned out to be of light skinned complexion. It was determined later that the mother had intimate relations at the same time with both Whistelo as well as a White man. Both the mother and father (Whistelo) stopped caring for this baby and ultimately left the child at an almshouse. The city of New York on behalf of the almshouse attempted to make Whistelo provide for his abandoned child.

In what should have been an otherwise routine paternity case, this trial became a case to determine the meaning of race. According to Timothy Messer-Kruse, the Whistelo Trial of 1808 "became a contest between popular and scientific theories of how race was inherited. Scholars have frequently cited the Whistelo trial as marking a turning point in the American scientific discourse surrounding race."[21] The Whistelo case offers a glimpse into how the social context of race helped formulate medical and scientific arguments about the racial differences of human beings. This case revealed how academic theories of the day understood how color and its perceived qualities transferred across generations.

The trial itself was historic in that it established a precedent on racial hierarchy, led by Columbia College's Samuel Latham Mitchell, a physician who testified that the flat nose and and thick lips of the baby confirmed it was black in spite of having light skin. This case ultimately led to how faulty racialized science was perpetuated by the academy. It was Dr. Samuel Latham Mitchell's testimony as an expert medical witness for the prosecution in the trial that solidified how science fit the anti-Black narrative. The testimony of physicians in the broader academy had justified setting a precedent for establishing a scientific explanation of race in America. The trial ultimately revealed how scholars weaponized science in order to engineer a consciousness to distinguish Black from White for the general population. This case also documents how scientists from the best institutions of higher education politicized science in order to justify racialized distinctions to benefit White people at the expense of Black people.

Wilder also writes how medical researchers at the nation's top academic institutions regularly conducted experiments on "colored corpses" in the

1800s, because there were fewer legal, political, and ethical restraints on the posthumous use of bodies of color. The White consciousness of scholars was either compartmentalized or nonexistent. Certainly their conduct indicated they did not consider Black bodies as equal in human worth as White bodies. Educators in the academy thus perpetuated a false narrative that reified the belief that Black lives had less inherent value. Indeed, from the inception of higher education in the United States, it appears that Black lives have never mattered.

It is not only through the production, codification, and distribution of knowledge that this racist agenda has been disseminated, it is also through the university environment. In Chapter 6, White Wrath, we documented some of the ways in which White supremacy groups are currently influencing the entire atmosphere of a campus. In spite of tropes about college education as a liberalizing force, there are strong elements of the campus climate that continue to cultivate White supremacy. One author compiled a list of six ways in which this still happens:

1. Faculty recklessly use the idea of "devil's advocate."
2. Advisers and mentors roll their eyes when discussing inclusion (treating efforts to rethink epistemologies as a nuisance communicates lack of value).
3. We discount students' voices (particularly student activists advocating for justice).
4. We fail to acknowledge that the world affects students.
5. We leave stereotypes about college unchallenged.
6. We fall into the trap of nostalgia.[22]

Some leaders love the idea of inviting diversity consultants to campus more than they love implementing the recommendations that result from the consultations. There are many more opportunities to deliver a keynote address on race than to conduct a diversity, equity, and inclusion audit. Many institutional leaders want the window dressing of diversity rather than actually dismantling racial injustice. In the best of cases, educational leaders implement workshops and trainings for faculty on racial microaggressions in the hopes that faculty might sound less racist in the classrooms, rather than with the goal of cultivating racial consciousness and becoming more anti-racist.

In workshops and seminars on anti-racism, we have used the analogy of home renovations to illustrate what is involved in dismantling systems of Whiteness. This begins with inspecting the very foundations of an institution.

I (Jun) recently completed a major remodeling project for my home, and having lived through this process, the analogy of home repair seems especially apt. My original goal for my home was simply to add a fresh coat of paint and new windows to my mid-century home in southern California. Upon the recommendation of a friend, I hired a general contractor. After a thorough diagnostic evaluation of my home, including a tour of both the basement and attic, he returned to deliver his assessment on the house. The bad news was that my house had significant and fundamental issues, including dry rot, an outdated electrical system, and antiquated plumbing and pipes that were rusty, leaking, and in desperate need of replacement. I was flabbergasted and immediately became distrustful of the contractor who came highly recommended.

Was he trying to rip me off? All I really wanted was new windows and paint. I wanted my house to look nicer and I wanted the affirmation from a professional that I did not have much to do. Instead, the contractor told me that I needed to address the structural integrity of the house. This expert contractor, with over thirty years of experience, was telling me that what I *really* needed was much more foundational, in areas that would not be immediately visible to others. It would take longer and cost more, but it was necessary and important work to do. The same is true for dismantling White supremacy in universities and other sectors of society.

What leaders *want* is the window dressing of diversity. What institutions *need* is to dismantle the foundations of supremacy. It will take a lot more time and cost a lot more money. Leaders will often balk at these recommendations. They prefer devoting an afternoon with faculty on addressing microaggressions in the classroom, or a plan to increase enrollment for students of color. These are not unimportant, but they are the equivalent to new windows and paint. These strategies fall short of addressing the deeper systemic issues that exist. The structure will continue to hurt students, faculty, and staff of color. These short-sided strategies ultimately hurt White colleagues as well, since the messages they are receiving about diversity are a superficial version of equity, which will lead to a need for further remedial education later.

If I responded to my contractor with denial that the home had such problems, or simply rejected his recommendations and insisted only on making the home look nicer, then foundational flaws to the structure would persist toward decay and destruction. In the same way, institutions that continue to reject the recommendations of equity scholars and that insist on superficial touch-ups in lieu of foundational changes are often left to deal with flareups, floods, and shit that overflows as a result of failing to address root causes. Again, roots will naturally bear the inevitable fruit.

White Consciousness Is Not Woke

The opposite of conscious is comatose, unaware, oblivious, uninformed, or asleep. However, when it comes to adapting the notion of critical conscious- ness to White structures and identities, the contemporary moniker "woke" does not apply. A White evolution toward racial justice is a perpetual state of mind and a constant state of being. "Woke" is past tense and indicates an arrival. In the case of White evolution, individuals and systems are either evolving one way or the other—toward supremacy or toward social justice. There is no neutrality, no stagnation, no plateau, no arrival, and no trophy. Any attempt at achievement or sense of arrival opens a person up to a turn back toward supremacy because of the pervasive nature of privilege and the White architecture of the mind.

There may be a natural temptation to go in search of badges of woke- ness and to be established as having moral authority by saying the right thing at the right time. But the truth is that racial consciousness has no "arrival" point. Hating Trump will not make anyone woke. Saying that you voted for Hillary Clinton will not make you woke. White tears and fake vulnerability over Whiteness will not make anyone woke. It simply indicates a desire for sympathy over accountability. Wearing a Black Lives Matter shirt will not make anyone woke. Illusive measures of wokeness likely will not lead to con- sciousness, because "woke" easily becomes an arrival point instead of a com- mitment to growth.

"The Great Awokening" is a term used to describe the movement of liberal White perspectives on the politics of race, following the election of Barack Obama through the election of Donald Trump.[23] Liberal White polit- ical viewpoints are now to the left of aggregate perspectives of people of color (according to surveys from the Pew Research Center and the *New York Times* General Social Survey). For example, White liberals have more positive feel- ings about immigration than those who identify as Hispanic; White liberals also attribute inequality to race more than people of color taking the surveys. Another example is a question that asks whether respondents agree or disagree with the statement, "Irish, Italians, Jewish, and many other minorities over- came prejudice and worked their way up; blacks should do the same without special favors." Half of liberal Whites disagreed, while only one third of Black respondents disagreed. White liberals may be a minority, but they are reshaping racial politics and the gap in polarization. According to one journalist:

> A big part of what Trump did in the 2016 campaign was simply increase the salience of racial conflict themes, thus boosting his appeal to white voters who may have previously backed Democrats on other grounds. But it's crucial to understand that, in large part because of the Awokening, Trump is not to blame: Democrats themselves have moved the goalposts in terms of what kind of racial views one is expected to affirm as a good liberal.[24]

The point here is that even if the goalposts move, it is still a game of winners and losers, or in a milder form, a system of compliance—neither of which is the same as racial consciousness.

Reaching a state of collective critical racial consciousness is a constant, never-ending project that requires continuous diligent excavation of self and society. Thus, the White *evolution* of the mind, in concert with a systemic ecological evolution, is a perpetual, incremental movement toward racial justice.

White Enlightenment Syndrome

White enlightenment syndrome happens when a White person is working to be woke by demonstrating how critical they are of other woke White people. It becomes a woke Olympics. In this regard, liberal White people are perhaps as dangerous as those who continue to exist unaware of racial inequities. Robin Di Angelo argues that White progressives can sometimes be the most difficult for people of color to deal with, because of the degree to which they think they have "arrived," they will put all their energy into making sure that others see them as having made it to wokeness.[25] This happens at the expense of putting energy into engaging in ongoing racial self-awareness and self-work, ongoing education, and genuine anti-racist advocacy and practices. This is what prevents cultivating consciousness and White evolution toward racial justice.

In his book entitled *Trouble I've Seen*, Black theologian and scholar Drew Hart shares about an exchange he experienced with a White colleague at a fast food restaurant. Hart's colleague placed a cup in the center of the table and proceeded to explain the mutual challenge of gaining any proper perspective from the standpoint of either side of the cup, as one side had a logo, and the other side had writing. Hart expressed gratitude to his well-intentioned

White colleague for offering this example, then proceeded to explain to him why this was ultimately a naïve way for White folks to understand racism. The analogy breaks down quickly, Hart went on to explain, because in fact he and other people of color *did* know what was on the other side of the cup. "This is because I learned Eurocentric history written from a white perspective. I have read white literature and poetry. I have learned about white musicians and artists. I have had mostly white teachers and professors through every stage of my educational process."[26] Hart juxtaposes his formal and informal educational experiences with that of his White colleague, who

> most likely could go through his entire life without needing to know Black literature, Black intellectual thought, Black wisdom, Black art and music, or Black history. That is, he could choose to never engage with or be changed by the range and beauty of the Black community. Nor would he be penalized for it.[27]

Hart's exchange with his colleague reveals much about the consciousness and evolution of Whiteness. Hart emphasizes that White people, in their eternal search for racial consciousness, are like societal explorers using telescopes with dusty lenses. These telescopes provide only a skewed view of what reality is for non-White others; and in their half-blinded discovery they often draw truncated and incomplete conclusions about people in non-dominant groups. They do so while insisting that their conclusions are accurate, scientific, logical, and natural. They will then tend to criticize other White people who also lean in with dusty lenses, and who draw similarly incomplete yet different conclusions about the social realities of people of color.

Conclusion

When we, as authors, consider our privileges over time, they present themselves as ailments with no known cure. We have different types of privilege, but they repeatedly reemerge. Like most chronic illness diagnoses, receiving such news is painful—but it can cultivate critical racial consciousness as a means to confront the disease. The treatment process will be painful. The procedures to help treat the disease may hurt more than the disease itself, because the illness is a silent killer. The moment we think we are in remission, we have a relapse. There will forever be a battle for the architecture of our minds. Interdependence is our strategy in the struggle for racial consciousness.

Just as racial categories were socially constructed out of an impulse to proliferate hierarchy and supremacy, we take those same constructions and recast them. By rewiring the architecture for supremacy through critical collective racial consciousness, the miseducation that has taken place through racist social structures can begin remediation.

Notes

1. Department of Justice Announces New Department Wide Implicit Bias Training for Personnel (June 27 2016). https://www.justice.gov/opa/pr/department-justice-announces-new-department-wide-implicit-bias-training-personnel.
2. Parker, Robert Dale. *Critical Theory: A Reader for Literary and Cultural Studies*. Oxford: Oxford University Press, 2012.
3. Hughey, Matthew W. "The (Dis) Similarities of White Racial Identities: The Conceptual Framework of 'Hegemonic Whiteness'." *Ethnic and Racial Studies* 33, no. 8 (2010): 1289–1309.
4. McClaren, Peter. "Critical Pedagogy: A Look at the Major Concepts," *The Critical Pedagogy Reader*, eds. Darder, Antonia, Marta Baltodano, and Rodolfo D. Torres (Hove, UK: Psychology Press, 2003), 61–83.
5. We acknowledge several scholars who have paved the way for our work, including Derrick Bell (see Bell, Derrick A. "Who's Afraid of Critical Race Theory." *University of Illinois Law Review.* (1995): 893) and Delgado and Stefancic (see Delgado, Richard, and Jean Stefancic. *Critical Race Theory: An Introduction.* New York: NYU Press, 2012); Gloria Ladson-Billings (see Ladson-Billings, Gloria. "Just What is Critical Race Theory and What's It Doing in a Nice Field Like Education?" *International Journal of Qualitative Studies in Education* 11, no. 1 (1998): 7–24); and Daniel Solórzano (see Lynn, Marvin, Tara J. Yosso, Daniel G. Solórzano, and Laurence Parker. "Critical Race Theory and Education: Qualitative Research in the New Millennium." *Qualitative Inquiry* 8, no. 1 (2002): 3–6).
6. Freire, Paulo, and Donaldo Macedo. *Pedagogy of the Oppressed.* New York: Bloomsbury Academic, 2018., p. 48–49.
7. Freire, p. 61.
8. Freire, p. 105.
9. Freire, p. 108.
10. Fanon, Frantz; Translated from the French by Richard Philcox. *Black Skin, White Masks.* New York: Grove Press, 2008. p. 161.
11. Hays, Danica G., and Catherine Y. Chang. "White Privilege, Oppression, and Racial Identity Development: Implications for Supervision." *Counselor Education and Supervision* 43, no. 2 (2003): 134–146.
12. Lechuga, Vicente M., Laura Norman Clerc, and Abigail K. Howell. "Power, Privilege, and Learning: Facilitating Encountered Situations to Promote Social Justice." *Journal of College Student Development* 50, no. 2 (2009): 229–244.
13. White, Sonny, Frankie Newton, Billie Holiday, Lewis Allan, and Billie Holiday, writers. *Strange Fruit.* Commodore, 1939, CD.
14. https://www.yesmagazine.org/peace-justice/stop-using-mental-illness-to-explain-white-supremacy-20170817.

15. Ibid.
16. King, Martin Luther, Jr. "Eulogy for the Victims of the 16th Street Baptist Church Bombing, 1963." Martin Luther King Jr. Scholars. June 19, 2015. Accessed May 07, 2019. https://mlkscholars.mit.edu/king-eulogy-1963/.
17. Noah, Trevor. *Born a Crime: Stories from a South African Childhood*. New York: Spiegel & Grau, 2019.
18. Yacovone, Donald. "How Scholars Sustained White Supremacy." The Chronicle of Higher Education. April 08, 2018. Accessed April 18, 2019. https://www.chronicle.com/article/How-Scholars-Sustained-White/243053.
19. "Teaching Hard History." Southern Poverty Law Center. Accessed April 18, 2019. https://www.splcenter.org/20180131/teaching-hard-history.
20. Wilder, Craig Steven. *Ebony & Ivy: Race, Slavery, and the Troubled History of Americas Universities*. New York: Bloomsbury Press, 2014.
21. Messer-Kruse, Timothy. "Humor and the Policing of the Boundaries of Racial Science: The "Remarkable" Whistelo Trial of 1808." *New York History* 96, no. 1 (2015): 9–37. https://muse.jhu.edu/ (accessed June 19, 2019).
22. Chatelain, Marcia. "How Universities Embolden White Nationalists." *The Chronicle of Higher Education*. August 17, 2017. Accessed April 18, 2019. https://www.chronicle.com/article/How-Universities-Embolden/240956?cid=rclink.
23. Yglesias, Matthew. "White Liberals Are Embracing Progressive Racial Politics and Transforming America." *Vox*. April 01, 2019. Accessed May 16, 2019. https://www.vox.com/2019/3/22/18259865/great-awokening-white-liberals-race-polling-trump-2020.
24. Ibid.
25. Di Angelo, Robin J. *White Fragility: Why It's So Hard for White People to Talk about Racism*. London: Penguin Books, 2019.
26. Hart, Drew G. I. *Trouble I've Seen: Changing the Way the Church Views Racism*. Harrisonburg: Herald Press, 2016. p. 25.
27. Ibid.

CONCLUSION

White supremacy is tenacious, portable, malleable, flexible, and insidious. It was built by White people, but because of its adaptability into psyches and systems, the present problem does not solely reside in White people. Accordingly, we try to advance a critique of White supremacy and White systems so as to not allow White people to be a distraction from the larger issue.

Whiteness always evolves. The concepts and critiques we introduced in this book represent some of the tools of White supremacy—especially in its more covert form. We name them in an effort to confront the racist logic systems hiding in the corners and shadows of both our minds and in social systems:

> Whitefluenza—dominance is like a disease with no known cure. It grows and manifests into supremacy, and it is hard to detect. A belief that the virus has been eradicated allows it to go untreated and unchecked. Recognition and commitment to collective active resistance is the first step in evolving racial consciousness faster than the virus.
>
> White 22—the belief that it does not really matter how hard you work on issues of race, you will always be inadequate: you are White if you do and White if you don't. The defeatist mindset serves to maintain White dominance both in individuals and throughout society.

White pain—a confusion between systemic injustice and individual injustice. Hearing about the personally experienced systemic injustices against people of color and equating them with one's own individual pain serves to conceal systems of racial injustice.

Whitroggressions—the assaults on and against White people that can instinctively lead to claims of reverse racism; perceived (and even felt) race-based individual shame and prejudice against White people. The concept is a misappropriated perception of personal offense with a failure to acknowledge structural racism.

White wrath—a reactionary response from the dominant group which fights back against efforts to curtail White dominance, and which maintains order through violence, rhetoric, activism, and policy.

White noise—the rationale, justifications, and excuses for Whiting out and explaining away systemic racial injustices. White static represents the ways in which the White power structure distorts logic to support the status quo, and White echo explains how White logic can operate in people of color. A White amplifier embodies and expands the ideology and logic of supremacy.

White consciousness—becoming critically aware of the White architecture of the mind and the dominant White logic systems in society. The notion of a collective critical racial consciousness includes the recognition of the importance of diversity for human flourishing and of evolution away from supremacy and toward racial justice.

Diversity is not the problem. Diversity is not the solution. Equity and racial justice require a collective effort to build anti-racism in a way that can overcome oppressive White logic. By identifying and naming the destructive elements of dominance, power, and supremacy, we can then begin to decode the logic of supremacy and evolve toward equity and justice.

It is difficult to focus on systems as both the problem and the solution, because systems are harder to grasp than individual behavior. Consequently, individualistic perspectives create a barrier to understanding the way systems work. In addition, intolerance for discussing a problem without the solution (a typical student disposition in a classroom setting) reinforces status quo problems. Learning to think systemically and dialogue about racial injustice requires *un*learning much of the dominant narrative that has been constructing the mental architecture of minds in schools, churches, and neighborhoods.

Two fundamental and underlying principles drove the writing of this book. The first was that the notion of evolution ought to be understood as a constant and intentional battle against the virus of supremacy. It is a race between supremacy and a critical collective racial consciousness. The second guiding principle was ecological. The genetic design of the human condition requires our interdependence in community. An ecological approach challenges some fundamental assumptions about the rugged individualism that is so revered in American society. The foundations of White supremacy are perpetuated by a reproduction of uniformity while increasing a fear of loss that comes with diversity. Ecological systems in nature often show that uniformity of any one substance can be detrimental to all other elements within the system. Monocultures are imbalanced and ultimately do not thrive. Diversity is needed for cultivation and flourishing. The supremacy of any one group with the hope of preserving the dominance of that one group is a threat to social ecology.

Cops, Koreans, and Race Riots

We recently heard a scholar (a person of color) speaking to a large audience on issues of race and White supremacy. One of the first questions was about acts of prejudice *among* communities of color. The scholar responded with a few comments about power, shades of color compared to Whiteness, and then said, "Not to be stereotypical, but…". As mentioned in the first chapter, the logic of the opener "Not to be…" is typically twisted. The speaker is about to say something that is indeed exactly what they appear to be disclaiming. The scholar went on to say, "I have been in convenience stores in Los Angeles where Korean shop owners are monitoring and following around Black patrons to make sure they don't steal." The potent combination of the "not to be" preface with a negative example of a Korean shop owner in LA, without any mitigating context or an attempt to point to the root problem, continues to veil the underlying architecture of supremacy. Even a scholar leading the way in anti-racism and racial justice activism can embody the very ideology they are trying to defeat. Racism is prejudice multiplied by power (addressed in Chapter 5 on Whitroggressions). When examining complex situations, we tend to ask the question, "Whose fault is it?" The purpose of the question is to embrace the complexity, and recognize that our logic is always incomplete. In order to evolve toward a critical collective racial consciousness, one must excavate. Excavation requires embracing the social complexity. And the struggle will remain constant.

There was a time in my life when I (Jun) wanted to became a cop. It was 1994 and the Los Angeles Police Department was looking to recruit. This was a particularly volatile period in the history of the City of Angels. There was the civil unrest in 1992 that has come to be known as the L.A. Riots.

Rodney King and the four officers who beat him were captured on video, but the four officers were found not guilty. I was in my early twenties and had already obtained a B.A. in psychology and political science, as well as an M.A. in counseling. I was contemplating the pursuit of Ph.D. in education, but I could not get rid of the mental images in my mind of seeing the L.A.P.D. let Koreatown burn.

Saigu is the English transliteration of 4/29 in Korean, which was the first day of the civil unrest. As I reflect back upon the L.A. Riots, nearly thirty years ago, I ask: Whose fault was this? I was working in Koreatown in the heart of Los Angeles at the Korean Youth and Community Center. I was an emerging social service worker interacting with Korean-American high school students, helping with drug prevention and gang intervention making $18,000 annually. Part of my responsibilities also included helping a few recent immigrants with limited English proficiency deal with bullying from Black classmates at predominantly Black high schools they attended in south central Los Angeles.

When the riots were first filmed at the intersection of Florence and Normandy on April 29, I had just returned from a site visit at a campus nearby. The four officers who were videotaped beating the late motorist Rodney King were acquitted, but in truth, what precipitated the riots was the death of teenager Latasha Harlins, an African American girl who was shot by a Korean-American immigrant in a liquor store. Latasha Harlins was reported to be stealing orange juice and items from the store on a regular basis. Soon Ja Du, the shop owner, looks like my aunt. The video surveillance shows Latasha Harlins grabbing Du by the hair and pulling her, then releasing her, and then walking out. Soon Ja Du reaches down, pulls out a gun and shoots Latasha Harlins in the back as she is leaving. Du was found guilty of voluntary manslaughter. The 16-year maximum prison sentence was averted and she was sentenced to probation, several hundred hours of community service, and a $500 fine.

The racial tensions between Korean and Black Angelinos had long been an issue before the *Saigu* riots. Ironically many of the perpetrators looting Korean stores in Koreatown were Latinx. Categorically, this is a byproduct of the construction and manifestation of a White architecture, designed to show a whole variety of people that they do not fit, and to blame each other for the feelings of not being fully accepted. This crabs-in-a-barrel phenomenon that pits communities of color against one another is itself a tragic manifestation of White supremacy. This has led to hatred, violence, and destruction. The obfuscation came in the form of hatred of different ethnic groups, rather than centering the problem on systems of White dominance and power that places oppressed groups against each other. Racial animosity between minority groups are certainly a concern and ought to be addressed, but not at the expense of ignoring the architecture and architects.

What most television audiences witnessed during the riots were Koreans pitted against Black and Latinx neighbors, with gun battles, looting, and buildings ablaze. The watching world also observed the Los Angeles Police Department essentially give up on Koreatown and south central L.A. in favor of protecting the richer, Whiter parts of the city. Police cordoned off the traffic at Hancock Park and the mid-Wilshire area which is the border of Beverly Hills. Whiteness manifests through the application of "protect and serve" as well as notions of "law and order."

In my first 20 years of life, prior to the riots, my experiences with police officers had only been positive. "Protect and Serve" had always meant that I felt safe and I trusted police officers growing up. This is part of the privilege I had as a light skinned non-Black person of color in an anti-Black society. Where I grew up, a dominantly White neighborhood in the San Francisco Bay Area, most of my classmates, neighbors, teachers, and police officers were White. Moreover, an unusually large proportion of my closer friends were sons of police officers. Those friends aspired to become police officers when they grew up, and the thought certainly crossed my mind a few times in my adolescence.

My first encounter with a police officer occurred when I was 15 years old. I was driving 55mph in a 25mph speed zone with my learner's permit, and my mom in the passenger seat next to me in our Oldsmobile station wagon. I heard the siren and saw the flashing light in my rearview mirror and my heart skipped a beat. The police officer approached and with a deep booming voice, demanded to see my license and registration. "Do you know why I pulled you over?" he asked, almost rhetorically. I gave him my learner's permit with a quivering hand. "I'm so sorry I was speeding ..." I was ready to explain, but upon looking at my permit his voice suddenly changed to a more lighthearted and jovial tone, and he asked, "Alex is that you?"

The officer was my friend's father. In fact, my friend was in the car with his dad on a ride along, and he was the one who caught me with the speed gun. The officer made small-talk with me and my mom, and then called my friend over. We had the friendliest time of catch-up on that residential street, the blue and red lights still flashing. This was my first experience of doing something that was legally wrong while simultaneously benefiting from a blue wall of protection at the age of 15.

From then on, I began to spend most of my time exclusively with friends whose fathers were cops. We engaged in all manner of inappropriate behavior as teenaged boys, regularly getting pulled over by the police, getting recognized, and simply reprimanded and ordered to return home. I was clever enough to learn the names and faces of my friends' fathers, and became close to many officers. All of this previous experience ended abruptly during the 1992 riots, when I finally saw Korean shopkeepers—people who look like me, my aunts, my uncles, my family, being denied both protection and service.

A year after the 1992 riots, as I was completing my M.A. in counseling, I decided to apply to the LAPD. My police interview did not go well. When my two White interviewing officers asked me why I wanted to join the LAPD, I replied that I never wanted to see the people of Koreatown left to fend for themselves again. I said that as a police officer I would uphold my duty to protect and serve. My other responses to interview questions were of the similar vein. From what I recall, I received a score of 90 out of a possible 100 on my interview. At the time, White and Asian applicants needed a score of 95 or better, while Black and Latinx applicants needed a score of 75 or better to qualify. This is what I was told as I was informed that I would not be invited to the Police Academy.

What does it mean to embrace multiple realities? At the time I could not fathom why Asian applicants were treated in the same way as White candidates, when the representation of Asians on the police force were as low as other ethnic minority groups. At the same time, I struggled with the fact that most of the brutal violence suffered by Korean immigrants in downtown L.A. occurred at the hands of Black and Latinx perpetrators, not White people. I confess that while growing up I had heard most of the older members of my Korean community express their disdain for darker skinned Black, Latinx, and Southeast Asian counterparts, and saw them strive to emulate *real* Americans—White people. We strove to be like White people (even echoes), we worked hard so we could move into their neighborhoods, attend their schools, lose our heritage language and culture to adopt theirs. We worked on our White game. All the while developing hatred toward other people of color, and ultimately hating and finding disgust in ourselves.

F. Scott Fitzgerald[1] once wrote that "The test of a first-rate intelligence is the ability to hold two opposed ideas in the mind at the same time, and still retain the ability to function." White dominant society creates conditions for people of color that erodes the possibility of solidarity. For some Asian Americans we are at once victims and perpetrators of racial animus toward people of other ethnicities.

A Way Forward

A viral video of Joy DeGruy Leary[2] lecture on Post Traumatic Slave Syndrome offers some salient points on racism. At one point in her seminar, DeGruy Leary asked the audience to raise their hands if they believe in White racism and again if they believe in Black racism. As hands stayed still, moved up, or moved slowly halfway up, the room became tense. Dr. DeGruy Leary then asked the participants how they could know the effects of White racism. Some of the answers included inequalities in education, healthcare, and other areas. She went on to ask how they can know the effects of Black racism. The room fell silent, and she explained the silence is due to the fact that it is the power behind White racism that leads to pervasive and real effects. Conversely, Black racism often carries some layers of disdain and even hate, but does not have the same influence on the ability to get a loan, or even on incarceration rates. Dr. DeGruy Leary explained that the only influence Black racism carries is fear. White logic perpetuates a fear of Black people. It is deeply psychological. Norm Stamper's[3] work revealed the extreme version of this fear among police officers. The bigger and darker the Black man, the more extreme the level of fear.

Although the individual experience is important, we have tried to create a vocabulary for understanding the White system in a new way. In doing so, we did not intend to provide a set of rules by which someone can confirm their status as a nice White person. We do not believe there is a set of rules to follow that will generate consciousness and acceptance. We are, however, convinced of the existence of a pervasive White system that can be seen, in part, through self-examination. But individual examination should not obscure the critical role of the dominant White system and its influence over the architecture of the mind.

Consider the following questions at a time when you have the space to process some of your own experiences, interactions, and ideologies:

How does White supremacist logic live within the architecture of my mind?
In what ways does White supremacy manifest in my thinking and action?

Do I tend to think in terms of individual action, or in terms of the ways in which social systems obstruct or enhance individual ability to navigate society?

Do I see the possibility of a radical commitment to an ecological and interdependent thinking that will alter the racial hierarchies embedded in our systemic logics and behaviors?

What will I do to outpace the White supremacist viral violence in my community and sphere of influence?

What are the results of a racial Rorschach test in my life. Is it a smile or a smirk, and has the ink blot evolved over time?

After I decode the White logic systems that have constructed the White architecture of my mind, what will I need to unlearn in order to evolve?

Who will be part of my collective, interdependent community that will lead to my evolution of racial consciousness?

I (Collins) enjoy stand up paddle boarding in the Pacific Ocean. Spaces inhabited by people are inherently racialized—from deserts to oceans and from suburbs to wilderness. On a warm day at the beginning of the summer of 2016, I was still learning to get in and out of the ocean with a giant paddle board and a paddle. If I was unable to time the incoming wave properly, my board, my paddle, and I myself would get tossed into the wave and churned all the way back to the beach. The same thing could happen when I was trying to get out of the water when I was done. After finishing a nice tour of the coast, I came out of the water and upon the sand and saw a mother and young boy watching me emerge out of the cool Pacific Ocean. The beach was empty except for the two of them. Fortunately, my timing was good, so I had not embarrassed myself in front of them. I smiled, picked up my board and started walking toward the road where I was parked. On the way, I passed a Black man who stood both taller and wider than me. As he passed, we exchanged a nod and kept walking. When he was about twenty feet behind me and headed down a path to the beach, he turned around and began to jog back toward me. I saw him out of my peripheral vision and bristled, tense, blood pumping, internal caution flags flying.

I tried to act like I was not experiencing fear. I do not remember exactly what he asked, but it was related to some curiosity he had about my paddleboard and a recounting of how he and his family were watching me paddle from the beach. I went back to the truck and loaded the board and sat down with ice water running through my veins wondering why. How has this fear been so deeply woven into my White psyche? It plays a key role in organizing the architecture of my mind. Society has shaped me and now I shape society.

My view of someone else can shape their self-understanding. The cycle of social construction is perpetual. The embedded ideologies of supremacy are tenacious and persistent. The more work I do in this area, the more I see the strength of status quo supremacy.

I (Jun) grew up admiring and paradoxically fearing adolescent White boys. As a shy, overweight sixth grader who had moved from a dominantly White elementary school to an equally dominantly White middle school in northern California, I was bullied regularly by a few of my Black and mostly White classmates. The Black boys were seen as disruptive both inside and outside of class, and everyone, including all of my White teachers, seemed to fear them. On the other hand, unlike the Black boys, the White boys were popular and well-liked by both students and teachers. Blonde-haired, blue-eyed, athletic and clean-cut, they were well-spoken and polite to teachers, coaches, and administrators. I recall most of them attending catechism classes on Wednesdays or going to temple on Saturdays.

Only recently have I realized how much many of them looked just like my co-author, Christopher Collins. In fact, many of the young White boys resembled characters I would see on television in the 1980s. Again, I admired them from a distance, and I recall trying to emulate their speech, mannerisms, and actions. However, I was taken aback and dismayed, heartbroken really, when these popular and well-regarded young White boys began to tease me and make fun of my hair, my eyes, and my yellow skin.

Microaggressive comments toward me in class, as well as outright racial insults verbalized in class, went unnoticed by my White teachers (who had proven their ability to hear every other inappropriate word uttered in class). I felt betrayed, and I wondered why people in authority did nothing to stop the pain I felt. I was not able to put into words, at the time, the systemic nature of it all. White boys who were popular had a sinister side to them, known only to a handful of select students of color who were victimized; teachers who represented power and authority in my life were silent in the face of racial injustice. Whenever I see young clean-cut adolescent White boys, I still feel that sense of distrust and recognize my own implicit biases toward them.

How does one disentangle, rewire, unlearn, and relearn? It cannot be done in isolation. The solutions will be as complex as the histories and experiences that created them. There is no panacea, quick fix, or silver bullet to eradicate embodied systems of supremacy. The evolutionary journey is long and constant.

Figure C.1: Collins in the Langa dompas museum in South Africa, photo taken by author

Globally White and Anti-Black

Whiteness is portable and can be seen on a global scale. Evidence of a system of Whiteness exists across the globe. Most systems of racial hierarchy are built around color, and lighter skin is almost always at the top. Figure C.1 is a picture taken in a dompas museum in the township Langa, just outside of Capetown, South Africa. In our next book, *White Diaspora: Universities and the Invasion of the Global South*, we explore the global nature of Whiteness. The confluence of virus-like privilege, the resistance to hearing the pain of others, feigning offense, feeling paralyzed, and staying angry comprise a stronghold of defense for White dominance. From skin Whitening creams to histories of colonial anti-Black policies, the concept of global Whiteness and anti-Blackness will bring another perspective on the evolving subject of White dominance and supremacy.

In *White Diaspora*, we explore White dominance in the Southern hemisphere through interviews with scholars and activists in South Africa,

Zimbabwe, New Zealand, Australia, and Brazil. We examine the earliest universities in these colonial outposts and the way in which Whiteness manifested with a different tenacity away from the White homelands of Europe. The historical and contemporary manifestations of Whiteness in these places are profound examples of supremacy.

We hope that by seeing, examining, acknowledging, and facilitating discussions about supremacy, we can begin the process of consciousness raising. We hope to find new architects of our own minds through solidarity and collective understandings of the human experience around the globe, and we encourage others to the same. We know that for many readers, the chapters included in this book have elicited strong reactions and opportunities for stretching. Our intent is to help transform and refresh others around the topic of racial justice.

Undoubtedly, there are some who have found much of this content to be quite challenging. We appreciate all who have persevered in this journey with us. For those who might turn away and disengage, never to return to these conversations again, who have been turned off by the way our writing has made you feel, due to our inability to convey a clearer and more winsome message, we express our regrets. However, for those who have experienced a transformation in thinking, there is an opportunity. The real work of evolution begins now, with those in your communities. The time has come to be bold and courageous. Despite the temptations to give up and give in, we must constantly persevere in the struggle.

Notes

1. Fitzgerald, F. Scott. "The Crack-Up." *Esquire*. October 06, 2017. Accessed June 04, 2019. https://www.esquire.com/lifestyle/a4310/the-crack-up/.
2. Mayweather, Cindi. "Black History Month—Post Traumatic Slave Syndrome by Dr Joy DeGruy Leary." *NeoGAF*. March 01, 2016. Accessed June 04, 2019. https://www.neogaf.com/threads/black-history-month-post-traumatic-slave-syndrome-by-dr-joy-degruy-leary.1188983/.
3. Stamper, Norm. *Breaking Rank: A Top Cops Exposé of the Dark Side of American Policing*. New York: Nation Books, 2006.

INDEX